THE WORLD OF THE BOTTLENOSED DOLPHIN

LIVING WORLD BOOKS
John K. Terres, Editor

The World of the
Bottlenosed Dolphin

David K. Caldwell
and Melba C. Caldwell

Illustrated with Photographs

J. B. LIPPINCOTT COMPANY

Philadelphia and New York

U.S. Library of Congress Cataloging in Publication Data

Caldwell, David Keller, birth date
  The world of the bottlenosed dolphin.

(Living world books)
Bibliography: p.

  1. Bottlenosed dolphins.   I. Caldwell, Melba C.,
joint author.   II. Title.
QL737.C432C27   599.5'3   71-159728
ISBN-0-397-00734-5   ISBN-0-397-00879-1 (Lib. ed.)

*Frontispiece: photograph by Nat Fain,
Marineland of Florida*

To
Jane Spottswood Keller Caldwell
and
George Danforth Caldwell
without whose constant encouragement over the
years we would never have gathered the data to
produce this book

Acknowledgments

WHEN ONE VISITS so many oceanariums and aquariums to gather first-hand material, picks the brains of so many catchers, handlers, trainers, and other people experienced with dolphins, and begs so many photographs and other kinds of help, it is hard to say just who did what and to what degree. Without any one of them this book would not be as complete as we have tried to make it. It is also dangerous to try to list completely those who have contributed, for in trying to do so one inevitably leaves out someone who was of special help. Nevertheless, we here list those who come to mind as having contributed something special to our effort. To those we have left out, it was purely an oversight and we apologize most sincerely: Earl J. Alford, Jr., Gary C. Ammons, Griffith Arrindell, Gregory Bateson, Charles Beckwith, Patricia Berger, Robert C. Boice, Winfield Brady, David H. Brown, Ricou Browning, Kent Burgess, Marie-Claire Busnel, René-Guy Busnel, D. J. Capo, D. R. Capo, Charles D. Carter, Burton Clark, Dewey Destin, Thomas G. DeVoe, Edward J. Doyle, W. H. Dukok van Heel, Albin Dziedzic, Richard Edgerton, Ken Engels, Donald S. Erdman, Jack Evans, William E. Evans, Natcher R. Fain, John E. Fitch, Jerry Foreman, F. C. Fraser, David E. Gaskin, Perry Gilbert, Hazel I. Hall, Nicholas R. Hall, Earl S. Herald, Paul Hirschman, Harry Hollien, Patricia A. Hollien,

Deane E. Holt, Don R. Hooker, William A. Huck, Donald R. Hurd, Blair Irvine, D. Scott Johnson, Fran Johnson, David W. Kenney, Judith King, J. W. LeBlanc, Sr., H. M. Lightsey, W. Fred Lyons, Barry McAlister, Frank J. McCallum, Peter Marler, Grady Marlow, J. Frank Miller, E. D. Mitchell, David A. Nelson, Masaharu Nishiwaki, Kenneth S. Norris, Barry Nutter, Ralph Penner, Thomas C. Poulter, Bill Powell, John H. Prescott, Warren F. Rathjen, William C. Raulerson, David W. Redman, Dale W. Rice, Sam H. Ridgway, William E. Schevill, Carl Selph, David E. Sergeant, J. B. Siebenaler, Marjorie Siebenaler, Armando Solis, Stephen H. Spotte, Nevin Stewart, Margaret C. Tavolga, William N. Tavolga, Colin K. Tayler, B. C. Townsend, Jr., Robert H. Turner, Cecil M. Walker, Jr., William A. Watkins, David Webb, Jesse R. White, J. Thomas Whitman, Carlotta Wilson, Clyde A. Wilson, Jr. II, Frank F. Wilson, F. G. Wood, Jr., James C. Woodard, Stephan G. Zam, and A. J. Zamba.

Much of our technical research has been supported by grants, contracts, and other financial or technical support, for all of which we are most grateful, from the following organizations: Office of Naval Research, National Science Foundation, National Institute of Mental Health, American Philosophical Society, U. S. Navy Marine Bioscience Facility at Pt. Mugu, California, Marineland, Inc. (Marineland of Florida), Gulf Exhibition Corporation (Florida's Gulfarium), Oceanarium, Inc. (Marineland of the Pacific), Aquatarium, Aquarium of Niagara Falls, Marine Exhibition Corporation (Wometco Miami Seaquarium), Sea World, Ocean World, and Biological Systems, Inc.

D.K.C.
M.C.C.

Contents

11

Perfect unison through the hoops. (Marineland of Florida)

Introduction

IN RECENT YEARS probably no single group of animals has caught the public eye as has the dolphin. Dolphins, or porpoises, or little whales, or whatever one might prefer to call these marine mammals, have been the subjects of books, magazine and newspaper articles, motion pictures, and television series and specials for several years now.

This mass public interest is a continuation and resurgence of an interest that man has had in these fascinating creatures for at least 2,500 years. We find remarkably good likenesses of dolphins featured on ancient Greek coins and pottery dating five centuries before Christ. Even older drawings recently found in South African caves show stylized dolphins and in at least one, a man is swimming nearby. Seamen have always regarded dolphins as good omens and friends, and it is remarkable how frequently these animals appear in the mythology of primitive island races, almost always in the role of potential ally to man.

Modern-day interest in dolphins probably began with the opening of the first trained-dolphin show in Florida in the late 1930's. Dolphins had been kept as aquarium specimens before; the famous P. T. Barnum even had a beluga (a kind of dolphin) that did some simple tricks in his American Museum in New York in the 1860's. But no one was aware that dolphins could be trained to do the things they can do until just after World War II, when Marineland of Florida (then called Marine Studios) reopened. It, too, had had dolphins as aquarium exhibits for several years before the war. It is hard to say just how the first training

13

Early photograph (circa 1939) of a dolphin jumping for food at Marineland of Florida, where dolphins were trained for the first time. (Marineland of Florida)

began, but many of the old-timers agree that it was pretty much by accident. Dolphins had been jumping for food and doing simple but related tricks at Marineland for some time, but one night Cecil M. Walker, Jr. (then a night pumpman and now assistant general manager), happened to notice that one of the bottlenosed dolphins seemed to be tossing a pelican feather toward him. Walker retrieved it and with patient coaxing developed this behavior pattern until the dolphin was tossing not only the feather but also such substantial objects as pebbles, rubber balls, and small inflated rubber inner tubes back and forth with him—or indeed with anyone else who would play. Step by step this simple game developed into the highly trained dolphin shows that can be found in widely scattered corners of the world today.

Introduction

The bulk of our book is devoted to the Atlantic bottlenosed dolphin, *Tursiops truncatus,* the most common species of dolphin of the inshore Atlantic waters of North America south of Cape Cod. The bottlenosed dolphin also lives in the Pacific and Indian oceans and their associated seas and gulfs, but it is a matter of record that most of the animals available for study, most of the biological data available from other sources, and most of the available photographs are of our Atlantic form.

Because the bottlenosed dolphin lives in inshore waters, often even in enclosed bays and marsh streams where space is limited and depths are shallow, it adapts well to captivity. Consequently, it is relatively easy to keep such captive individuals in good health if they are given proper attention. The grace and agility of dolphins at sea, long familiar to most seafaring men, are now combined with their breathtaking ability to perform, and their feats never cease to create wonder and excitement in the beholders.

Dolphins are extremely responsive to humans and show so much individuality in their behavior that it is often impossible, even for people

This young dolphin, Twothirtytwo by name, uses every trick to entice humans to play. Here he was especially successful and even got his trainer Nick Hall into the tank. (David K. Caldwell)

who use them as experimental subjects, to remain aloof. Such behavior on the part of dolphins, along with their intelligence, soon tends to lead the unsuspecting and noncautious observer astray, and before he knows it he may tend to think of them as people. We ourselves have a young male dolphin (housed at Marineland of Florida) that has learned every trick in the book to get humans to play with him. His tank is so situated that many of the Marineland employees, all delivery trucks, and even occasional tourists pass by it. This causes considerable trouble, because the animal is in training for sound discrimination studies for the Navy and should not have contact with outsiders. But he is irresistible, and so we are really forced to chase away the people he lures to the side of his tank.

To the scientific community the dolphin has always been much more than just another animal that plays and can be trained to do tricks on command. Behavioral studies of the bottlenosed dolphin have intrigued us for many years because they offer potential insight into comparative studies with land mammals, particularly in social behavior. Dolphins are a gregarious and obviously advanced species whose ancestors took to an aquatic environment more than 45 million years ago. Some facets of their social behavior should show gross differences between land and sea mammals, indicating that widely different solutions to behavioral problems are workable. Conversely, if this species has evolved (or retained) a solution that closely resembles one arrived at by similarly advanced terrestrial mammals, such as primates (man, apes, monkeys, marmosets, and lemurs) or wolves, we may speculate that perhaps this may be the "best" solution. It may even be the only solution.

Scientists have been investigating the feasibility of the sea as a long-term habitat for man. It now appears certain that man can live and work underwater for several weeks, but many problems need solving in order to make life easier and safer for him. It is hoped that dolphin research will provide insights into these problems. For example, man's ability to locate and identify objects diminishes as his vision becomes less effective in the underwater darkness. Because dolphins use sound to resolve this crucial problem, the manner in which they do so—known as echo-location (a kind of sonar)—is presently under intensive study by several investigators.

Communication between human divers, and between them and their habitat or support ship presents another problem because radio waves do not travel well underwater. Here again, scientists are taking a good hard look at solutions reached by dolphins over the millennia.

Unfortunately, much of the recent popular literature on dolphins tends to portray them as "little men in wet suits." A lot of attention has been centered on the notion that dolphins are as smart as some men, or smarter than most, or that they can talk but that we humans are just too stupid to understand them. It is true that some have worked un-tethered with aquanauts in the Navy's Sealab programs; however, dolphins probably are just exceptionally amiable mammals with an intelligence now considered by most workers, on a subjective basis, to be comparable to that of a better-than-average dog. We think this is about as complimentary a statement as can be made about any mammal.

In the long run all this controversy has had a positive effect. People have had a fine time debating just how smart dolphins really are, and scientists have been prompted to study dolphins, using careful experimental methods. As a result, a whole new field of mammalian research has developed and continues to expand. Because dolphins live in water and don't have appendages like hands or a true language as man understands that word, it is difficult to measure their intelligence. But it is also difficult to measure man's intelligence, for we really don't know what "intelligence" is. And even if we did know, it would be difficult to make comparative studies. When we speak of "intelligence" in dolphins or dogs or monkeys, it is a matter of subjective thinking. Our feelings have a lot to do with this, and for now our comparisons of intelligence are limited by this very unscientific technique. We hope that someday we can do better.

17

There is still much to learn about bottlenosed dolphins, especially details of their anatomy and physiology; but, considering the difficulty of obtaining data, because dolphins are difficult to obtain these days (due to more stringent laws regarding capture, increased costs for collection, and ever-increasing public opinion against their capture), we know a surprising amount already—particularly about their behavior and natural history. For this reason we can make realistic generalizations in the following chapters—as long as the reader understands that to explain the gaps and exceptions in detail would go beyond the limits of this book.

Because the full common name of the species, the Atlantic bottlenosed dolphin, is such a mouthful, we will refer only to dolphins. Whenever we make comparisons with other species of dolphins, porpoises, or whales, we will fully identify the animals we are discussing.

Meet the Dolphin

BEFORE DELVING INTO the dolphin's world, we would like to make a few general comments. The dolphin is a warm-blooded, air-breathing mammal that bears its young alive and suckles them for a year or more before they are fully weaned. The average dolphin is gray, but not the flat gray usually depicted. It often has some very distinctive markings, albeit these, too, are shades of light and dark gray with a touch of creamy white in places. The sexes are essentially indistinguishable externally when viewed from the dorsal (back) surface, but this subject must be studied further because a few fishermen tell us that they can tell the sexes apart without examining the ventral (under) side of the animal. Ventrally, the distinction is easy since the female has only one obvious vent, whereas the male has two.

At birth, dolphins measure about 3½ feet in over-all length and weigh about 30 pounds. The average dolphin that one sees in a show or otherwise on display is between 7 and 8 feet long and weighs perhaps 300 to 400 pounds. While some of these animals are adult, many are not, and much larger individuals—some of them up to 10 feet long and weighing as much as 850 pounds—are seen in our western Atlantic. In European waters, individuals of this species commonly exceed this length by as much as 2 or more feet, with an equivalent increase in weight.

19

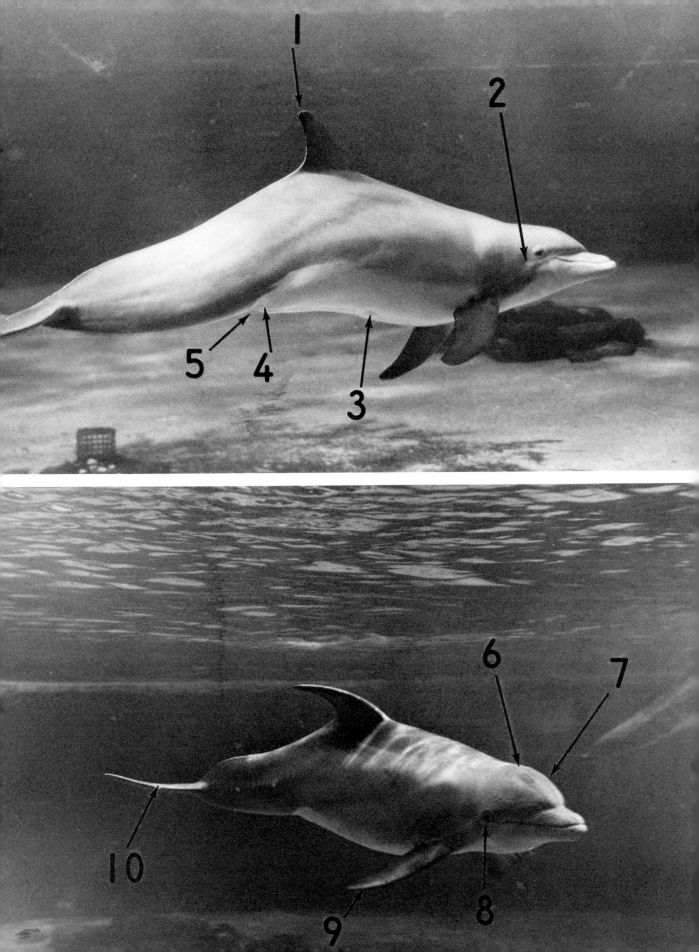

In general, dolphins eat fishes, which they swallow whole, almost invariably head first, using their sharp conical teeth only for grasping. They seem to have few enemies after they reach adult size and, with few possible exceptions, should not be considered either enemies to man or competitors in his fishing and sporting activities. Dolphins are very vocal and extremely social, and it is fortunate that they continue to remain so in captivity, for we can study them with greater ease and reliability.

Dolphins have certain features that are unique to cetaceans and other mammalian features that may be unfamiliar to the general reader. As a guide to some of these, we have labeled two photographs of different adult females in captivity. Top left: (1) dorsal fin, (2) external auditory meatus, or external ear opening, (3) umbilical scar, (4) one of two mammary slits, the other is in the same position on the other side, (5) genital region, including the excretory openings and vaginal opening, all in one medial slit (in the male, only the anus is located here while the penis is withdrawn within an opening forward of this). Bottom left: (6) blowhole, located just to the left of the midline, (7) melon, overlying the skull, (8) eye, (9) pectoral flipper, homologous with the human arm, (10) flukes, or tail, a feature unique to certain aquatic mammals and not homologous to the human leg. Note the piles of rocks on the bottom of this tank, in which the dolphins perform by jumping for food. Apparently the animals use these as guideposts to position their jumps, for if the rocks are moved the animals become disoriented in their jumping for a short time until they learn new landmarks. (Marineland of Florida)

A true porpoise lies on the deck of a ship in eastern Canadian waters. (Audio Visual Sciences Department, University of Guelph)

A strikingly marked eastern Pacific killer whale seems to leap for joy. (Marineland of the Pacific)

Dolphins, Porpoises, and Whales

ONE OF the more frequent questions we are asked is: "What is the difference between a dolphin and a porpoise?" Actually, there is no biological confusion; the problem lies in semantics, brought about—as is often true in many fields—by the long-time and worldwide use of common names in referring to these animals. The differences between these two marine mammals are not obvious to the layman, and not always so even to the casual technical observer. Most people in America call dolphins "porpoises," and only the most technical will argue in conversation, although they probably would do so readily in print.

Dolphins, according to the majority of scientists, are cetaceans (whales, dolphins, and porpoises all belong to the major taxonomic group Cetacea), in the family Delphinidae. Members of this group are best characterized by having conical (cone-shaped) teeth, an obvious snout or beak that is sharply demarcated from the forehead, and a dorsal fin that usually is hooked at the tip. But already we are in trouble, because although the teeth of all dolphins are conical, some dolphins don't have an obvious snout (like the familiar pilot whale, for example) and others don't have a dorsal fin at all. There are also fresh-water dolphins that are quite different from their marine cousins and have their own set of rules, which don't really apply here.

Porpoises, again according to most biologists, belong to the cetacean family Phocoenidae. Members of this family are best characterized by

23

teeth that have a spadelike crown and are laterally compressed (flattened on two opposing sides) and no obvious snout. The porpoise's dorsal fin is usually triangular in shape like that of the dolphins but not hooked (it is more obviously a triangle than a sickle like the dolphins'). However, there are exceptions here too, for some porpoises also have no dorsal fin.

It is therefore easy to see why there is so much confusion on the part of the layman. The problem may never be resolved, and so the writer or speaker should always make it very clear to the audience just what kind of "dolphin" or "porpoise" is meant.

Whales versus Dolphins and Porpoises. We encounter similar problems in semantics when we try to distinguish between "whales" and "dolphins and porpoises." In general, the term whale seems to be applied to any large cetacean, no matter what its true relationships to the other members of the group.

There is never any argument about the members of the order Mysticeti, which includes all of the large baleen whales (ones that, instead of teeth, have masses of horny plates with feathery edges, to strain food from the water, hanging down from the roof of the mouth).

Among the toothed whales (order Odontoceti), the mighty sperm whale clearly deserves the designation, but other members of the same family (the Physeteridae), the pygmy and dwarf sperm whales, are relatively small—although scientists are usually in agreement in calling them whales, probably out of respect to their huge cousin. The beaked whales (family Ziphiidae) are often dolphin- or porpoise-like in their body form; being large, however, they are also usually called whales. On the other hand, members of the Arctic family Monodontidae—the beluga or white whale and the narwhal—are called whales despite their being the size of dolphins.

So far, so good (or so bad). However, when we get into the odontocete family Delphinidae we really find ourselves in trouble with semantics.

24

A dolphin fish bears no real resemblance to a dolphin mammal. (Marineland of Florida)

An eastern Pacific pilot whale, or blackfish, completely clears the water to bump a ball. (Marineland of Florida)

Usually the larger species, even though they may be dolphins, often pass for killer whales, false killer whales, and pilot whales. Then there is the rare species called the pygmy killer whale, which is the size of a dolphin. It probably gets its whale tag by riding the coattails of its more impressive cousins with which it shares an imposing set of teeth. We can sum up the situation by saying that usually size dictates the use of "whale" instead of "dolphin." If we try to be more specific, we get into problems such as this: pilot *whales,* technically *dolphins,* are often called black*fish.*

Another source of confusion is the fact that there is a well-known marine game *fish* called a dolphin — but only the name is confusing. The dolphin fish has a tail that lies in a vertical plane; the dolphin mammal's tail lies in a horizontal plane — and this alone is enough to quickly distinguish a true fish from a cetacean. There are many other broad differences between the two: fishes are cold-blooded (that is,

25

their body temperature varies with that of the surrounding environment); mammals are warm-blooded (their body temperatures are relatively constant no matter what the temperature of the surrounding environment); fish have scales but no hair at any stage of their lives, mammals (even dolphins) always have at least a few hairs at some stage; fish do not nurse their young with milk, mammals do; and so on.

It is truly hard to suggest what one should do when applying common names to cetaceans. We have no suggestions except to try to follow the middle of the road, and again to be sure the reader is clearly aware of the animal being discussed. The only sure way to do this is to include the scientific name somewhere near the beginning of a discussion. Under the laws of taxonomy, a scientific name (usually of Latin or Greek origin) applies to only one kind of animal, and is applied and understood around the world in whatever language is being used.

A newborn dolphin still has a few mammalian hairs on its snout, but will lose them very rapidly and retain only the follicles for the rest of its life. (Natural History Museum of Los Angeles County)

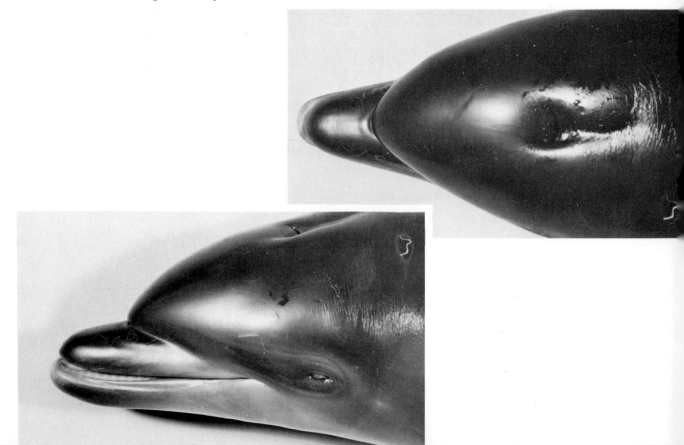

Dolphins, Porpoises, and Whales

Bottlenosed Dolphin Subspecies. The genus *Tursiops,* to which our bottle-nosed dolphin belongs, is in such a state of taxonomic confusion at present that it would serve little purpose to say much now about other species. There are about a dozen other named species of bottlenosed dolphins, but most, if not all, of these are almost surely synonyms for three forms, all of which may merely be subspecies of the species *truncatus.* There is even some question that these three should be separated. Members of the genus *Tursiops* are widely distributed in temperate and tropical seas around the world and about such mid-ocean island groups as Hawaii, even though it is generally considered a rather shallow-water, shore-loving group.

Although the bottlenosed dolphins on both sides of the Atlantic bear the same specific name, *Tursiops truncatus,* this arrangement must be questioned because we in Atlantic America almost never see bottlenosed dolphins as large as those commonly taken in European waters (including the Mediterranean Sea). By the same token, European aquarists rely mostly on American suppliers for their bottlenosed dolphins because the ones in their local waters are too large to handle conveniently. There is much room for study in the problem of "most common size" between American and European bottlenosed dolphins. Whether the variation is due to ecology, life history, or real genetic population differences of taxonomic rank is as yet unknown.

There is still some question concerning the taxonomic placement (classification) of the eastern Pacific bottlenosed dolphins. Some scientists believe that two species may be involved there: Our *Tursiops truncatus* and one usually called *Tursiops gilli* (although some writers refer to this latter form as *Tursiops truncatus gilli*). *Tursiops gilli* is said to be somewhat larger and darker in color than *Tursiops truncatus,* but this is a matter of conjecture because large individuals of *Tursiops truncatus* live in the Atlantic and some of these seem to be darker on the average than others. Interestingly, a light-hued Atlantic animal was taken to Hawaii for a research project, and it gradually turned the typical dark color of

27

High-jumping dolphin, possibly Tursiops truncatus aduncus, *from eastern Australia. (Marineland of Australia)*

Tursiops gilli after spending some time in the bright tropical sun in a shallow holding pool containing especially clear water. After its return to the mainland and more subdued sun and less clear water, it lightened in color again—apparently it changed "species" with the changes in degree of suntan. The form native to Hawaii is believed by most scientists to be *Tursiops truncatus*.

Most writers consider the possibility that a form of bottlenosed dolphin from the tropical Indo-Pacific may be a third recognizable form that should be accorded subspecific rank. If so, it would be known as *Tursiops truncatus aduncus,* as opposed to *Tursiops truncatus gilli* in the eastern Pacific (in part), and *Tursiops truncatus truncatus* in the remaining regions where the genus is found.

Most of the captive bottlenosed dolphins one sees in America and Europe come from Florida, or at least their parents did. For a time it was believed that the ones from our East Coast waters were more easily trained; therefore animals from the east were shipped west. After having had more opportunity to attempt to train individuals of their own local

Before getting into harness, a dolphin "horse" makes sure its passenger is securely aboard. (Marineland of Florida)

form, some trainers on the West Coast now dispute this difference, but the argument still rages and for this reason animals for the most part continue to be shipped from Florida. The same is true for Europe, where the local animals are reported to be "duller" in intelligence than the ones imported from Florida, and shipments to that continent continue as well as to the Pacific coast and to Hawaii. Whatever the reasons, whether real or fancied, the fact remains that most of the bottlenosed dolphins appearing in shows on the West Coast of America and in Europe, and the majority used for research there, originally came from Florida or nearby Mississippi. Consequently, although we would like to say more about Pacific-originated bottlenosed dolphins, the material to do so is just not available at this time. The available limited data on the named forms *gilli* and *aduncus* indicate that the two forms seem to be pretty much the same in their biology as *truncatus*. We see no real reason for the purported differences in behavior, but do know that many trainers continue to stick to their convictions that *Tursiops truncatus truncatus* is the most trainable.

29

Two large females swim with their sons as a family group. The calf shown second from the right is just over a year old, while the one on the far left is just a few months of age. (David K. Caldwell)

Dolphin Community Life

ONLY IN OCEANARIUMS with communities of captive dolphins can either scientists or interested laymen regularly and conveniently observe a semi-natural colony of these aquatic mammals as they play, fight, form deep bonds of affection, reproduce, rear their young, and perhaps even die of old age. Most oceanariums have large tanks, usually with underwater viewing ports for watching the animals, and here, in the clear filtered water, most scientists go about their work of studying dolphins. Constant, long-term observations of relatively undisturbed dolphin communities must be carried out before intelligently directed experimental work can begin.

There must be sufficient space in the tanks to permit relatively normal interactions between several individuals of assorted sizes and sexes. Tanks with a desired diameter of 75 or more feet and a depth of 10 or more feet are available at fewer than a dozen places—all of them in the United States, as far as we know. To our knowledge the establishments in other parts of the world that have imported American dolphins do not have the required study facilities, and the ones that do have such tanks for the most part display different kinds of dolphins and porpoises. Consequently, despite the popularity and frequent exhibition of Atlantic bottlenosed dolphins there is a limited number of places where good studies of community behavior can be made.

We will compare observations made in captivity with the little that is

31

known about the natural history of this species in the wild. At this point we can say that the rare observations in the wild indicate a close similarity in behavior with that seen in captivity. Generally, only those behaviors such as formation of sub schools and home range that require tremendous space not available in captivity have varied between those in captivity and those in the wild.

Infants and Juveniles. Oceanariums have met with considerable success in rearing dolphins born in captivity. At Marineland of Florida, this success has been carried to the point where two generations have been born from a mother brought in from the wild.

The gestation period in dolphins is about eleven to twelve months. Birth is usually rapid, taking place in less than an hour after hard labor begins. During this time the other dolphins often show intense interest, and there have been cases where it has been suspected that the other animals aided in delivering a calf in a birth that was not going well, but this has not been confirmed. Normally, the other dolphins give no direct assistance. Those births taking much longer than an hour usually result in the calf being stillborn.

Two adult female eastern Pacific whitesided dolphins closely attend the delivery of a bottlenosed dolphin. (David K. Caldwell)

Light-colored fetal folds still mark this infant female. (Marineland of Florida)

Dolphins are normally born tail first. A newborn calf is almost a duplicate of the adult in shape; it is only about one third as long as the mother and is usually somewhat darker. On its sides are several narrow light-colored bars which are believed to be the result of fetal folding when the unborn dolphin is still slightly curled within its mother's womb. These bars are very obvious for the first few weeks and clearly signal the newborn young. Although the bars may last for several months, they are faint after the first few weeks and may show up only in a favorable light.

Immediately after it is born, the calf swims to the surface on its own to take its first breath of air. The mother follows closely behind, but motion pictures of this fast action show that she does *not* assist the newborn calf to the surface, as has so often been written. However, if the calf falters or is in real distress, or is stillborn, the mother attempts to help it to the surface. It is next to impossible to separate a mother from her dead calf, and in the wild, mothers have been found carrying their dead and decomposing young for several days.

The calf follows its mother from the moment of birth. It has no prob-

This young calf, only a few weeks old, sticks close to its mother. (Marineland of Florida)

The mother dolphin, known as a cow, turns on her side and reduces her swimming speed to allow her infant calf to nurse. (Marineland of Florida)

lem keeping up with her because it is both lifted and carried along by the hydrodynamic forces of water moving in a stream past the body of the adult. In a sense, the calf is carried along in an envelope of moving water generated by the larger adult. This "echelon swimming," as it is called sometimes, takes place almost regardless of how fast the mother swims, and the young calf can keep up with its mother and the school with essentially very little effort, even on sharp changes of course.

Judging from our personal observations, the young calf does not begin to nurse successfully until the female expels the placenta. This may not occur for several hours, although it sometimes happens within an hour after birth. Before placental expulsion, the calf makes exploratory nursing attempts, usually at the wrong places, which include the mother's head, neck, flukes (tail), and flippers. After the placenta is expelled, the mother appears to direct the infant's efforts by rolling her body and adjusting her swimming speed so that the infant's snout engages one of the two mammaries (each of the two nipples is in a slit parallel to the single genital slit of the female). The calf nurses at frequent short intervals for the first six months or so of its life, receiving an extremely rich milk believed to be squirted into its mouth along a tube formed by the infant's troughlike tongue and the mother's nipple. The calf grows rapidly on this diet and begins to take a few fishes when it is about six months old, although it may also continue to nurse for a year or more.

Observers have noted that the mother sometimes prevents the calf from feeding on fishes at too early an age, and that she may break off the heads of the first ones it is allowed to eat—an act that would prevent the infant from swallowing the larger bones of the fish. The calf's teeth begin to erupt at about this same time, and at first year's end the youngster is able to grasp fishes on its own. By now it assumes the nursing position only when alarmed by some apparent danger or otherwise disturbed. For example, a male dolphin slightly over a year old resumed nursing for a short time when a calf was born to another female in the community at Marineland of the Pacific.

The newborn infant seems to sleep frequently for periods of about 1 to 5 minutes, usually after nursing. The eyes close and all motions cease except those which are necessary for swimming alongside the mother and surfacing occasionally for air. These naps continue, but at diminishing frequency, during the first year; after this the juveniles, as far as we have been able to determine, appear to regard sleep as a waste of good playtime.

Although the young dolphin may stay with its mother for as long as a year and a half, it begins to venture away from her to explore its immediate surroundings when it is just a few weeks or months old. When real or potential danger threatens, the mother often has to come after her wandering calf, which may incite the infant to a game of chase. There have been times when severely tried mothers have punished calves by biting at them or even forcibly holding them on the bottom of the tank for a few moments. Following the latter punishment especially—during which the calf often does considerable struggling and vocalizing—it seems duly chastened and takes its position beside its mother for some hours to come.

There is good evidence that the dolphin mother and her calf are sometimes joined by another adult female called an "auntie." Lions and elephants are also known to make use of aunties, and the association appears

A cow is quick to punish her half-grown son when he tries her patience too far. (David K. Caldwell)

A very young calf surfaces to breathe (or "blow") while flanked by its mother and auntie. (Marineland of Florida)

to be one of helping to care for and protect the young. The calf sometimes goes off with the auntie, and the real mother does not appear to object, although she keeps watch over them. In captivity the auntie may even be a different kind of dolphin.

Young dolphins engage in considerable play as do many juvenile mammals. Playing usually involves nosing or carrying some object around; but it may also become more complex. Some games involve chases with other young dolphins, or even adults. In captivity the young may also play with other kinds of dolphins. Teasing by using objects as bait is frequent and is preceded by clear-cut signals of invitations to play. One animal swims slowly up to another, dangling the object between its teeth. The object is offered more and more closely and freely until the invitation is accepted and the chase is on. The play is not restricted to chasing and teasing, for the juveniles are very adept at developing new games. Sometimes these activities become a problem to humans working with the animals. On two occasions, with two different juvenile male dolphins, we have had the animal deliberately toss our dangling hydrophone (underwater microphone) out of the tank when we were trying to record sounds.

37

One of these juveniles uses every opportunity and every trick of the trade to get humans to play. On one occasion, a night watchman making his rounds did not see the dolphin as he passed by the tank. As any good watchman should do, he directed the beam of his flashlight into the dark water to try to see the animal, fully expecting to discover that he had either been stolen or was lying dead on the bottom. Instead, the dolphin, appearing seemingly out of nowhere, grabbed the flashlight from the watchman's hand and swam away with it. Somewhat angry but relieved to find the animal still there, the watchman got a long-handled net and tried to retrieve his light. Each time he got close to it, the playful dolphin pushed it away. This went on for some time before the ruined flashlight was recovered. This same dolphin often offers a small floating rubber ball to anyone passing by and, if the person accepts it, will play a game of retrieve until the poor human is exhausted. Sometimes he offers an uneaten fish, and this game may go on with the dolphin alternately sucking in and spitting out the fish until it is a total shambles.

Young dolphins even play with their own sounds. While listening to the sounds being recorded from a community tank we have all at once heard some very strange noises come though our earphones. Looking through the viewing port, we have observed a small juvenile male lying motionless in mid-water obviously making different sounds (as evidenced by the emitted bubbles from his blowhole*) for no apparent reason other than play. It is not unusual for human juveniles, or even adults, to do this—so why not dolphins? The same sort of behavior has been demonstrated by the precocious dolphin that likes to provide night watchmen with extra activity.

Much of the behavior of captive dolphins is obviously sexual. Although some writers have postulated that this is due to confinement in cramped quarters, observations made in the wild from underwater

---

* Editor's Note: The blowhole is the anatomical equivalent of nostrils in a human being and its use is explained by the authors in the chapter, "Sensory and Communication Processes," pp. 97–122.

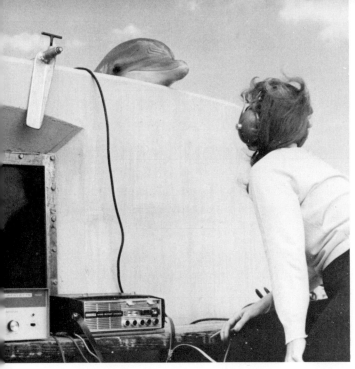

Twothirtytwo again. This time he appears more interested in the observer than in making sounds for Melba to record. (Marineland of Florida)

vehicles have shown clearly that a comparable amount of sexual behavior takes place in wild herds. The development of sexual behavior in dolphins then is a very important part of their over-all behavioral pattern. Dolphin customs in the matter of socially acceptable sexual behavior would not meet with those imposed by our society. Neither, however, do they need psychiatrists to analyze their sexual problems. We would like to go on record here as stating that we have never recorded a single embarrassed sound from a dolphin tank but a great many giggles from human bystanders.

Fortunately for the ultimate attainment of knowledge, the human mind is so constituted that it needs to categorize everything. However, at times we all forget that our understanding of nature itself has not advanced to the point where we can do such compartmentalizing. This is especially true of sexual behavior and its development. Who can say today at what given moment the word "play" should be exchanged for "affection" or "sex"? In dolphins, just as youthful play-chasing at times and in time leads to fight-chasing, which in turn leads to the establishment or defense of territories, so nuzzling at its mother's nipples leads the infant to inexperienced attempts at mating and eventually to the development of all components of sexual behavior.

39

Dolphins in captivity do not begin to attain sexual maturity until they are six or seven years old, and in the wild it may take twice as long. There is, then, a long period of sexual exploration, play, and experimentation. These patterns begin to develop almost from the hour that the calf starts to nurse, becoming overt when it begins to actively and forcefully play just a few weeks after that.

Infant male dolphins that we have observed have all attempted to mate with their mothers within a few weeks of birth. Nuzzling of the mammary glands apparently at times stimulates the mother, and we have frequently observed her taking the initiative in sexual activities. By the time he is a year old the male has learned what appears to be the full adult mating pattern, and has practiced with most of the females in the community tank.

Although we have access to newborn and juvenile females, they were not in a tank that permitted detailed observation of the development of sexual behavior. Even if we had had good viewing, their anatomy is such that arousal is not as obvious as with a male and the development of this behavior could not be studied in them as readily. It probably is not as complicated as that of the male, but most likely also begins at an early age.

In addition to heterosexual relationships, older juveniles and young adults of both sexes engage in both self-stimulation and homosexual behavior, and switch freely from one to the other. In adults, heterosexual relationships become predominant.

In some large-brained mammals (humans, some monkeys, and certain seals, for example) a dominant male may subject a less dominant male to a homosexual act, solely as an expression of superiority and connoting physical aggression rather than sexuality. We have seen homosexual behavior of this nature in dolphins only once. On that occasion the dominance gesture took place when a larger adult male was introduced into the home territory of a subadult male in a dolphin community tank containing females as well as dolphins of other species. After approxi-

Two subadult males work out their socialization problems in an effective manner. (David K. Caldwell)

mately 30 minutes of sizing up each other, the larger male apparently decided that he could be boss of that outfit, even though he had the disadvantage of being a newcomer, and proved it by subjecting the smaller one to several homosexual performances. The matter was apparently settled once and for all, because the dominant dolphin never did this after the first day.

Socialization and Aggression. From our observations and those of others, it is apparent that growing dolphins learn much about sex from adult females. From the adult males they surely learn threat signals, flight, and perhaps visually acquired aggressive techniques. Their relationships with others in their peer groups also teach them much about the ways of life; in their play and presexual activities they undoubtedly establish hierarchical relationships with those in their herd.

Over a period of years the socialization process changes from the almost total permissiveness extended to the infant to the virtually total retaliatory attitude extended by adults to other adults in their society. For social animals such as dolphins and humans, growing up involves taking a few blows; the previous infantile appearance, gestures, and phonations, which elicited care from adults, are now gone forever. The former infant that was reprimanded by a gentle nip suddenly finds that

41

an overly aggressive act of teasing an adult results in a full-blown slap from the adult's flukes. Should a young male dolphin approach a female sexually, he may receive the full force of a slashing bite from a more dominant male.

The maturing male now begins to acquire some cautiousness in his approaches to strange animals or objects, albeit a caution that is quickly and easily overcome by an obvious eagerness to investigate more closely. He learns the difficult ambiguous signals of *play* versus those of *seriousness* given by members of his society. That this learning is not acquired without some pain is demonstrated by the cuts, scrapes, and bite marks the dolphin accumulates as he engages in active play with other individuals of his kind.

He also is learning that he is not without power in his own teeth and flukes, and acquiring some judgment as to when to exert it and when to retreat. Usually the opponent's size is the deciding factor. In captivity, it sometimes becomes necessary to remove maturing males from a tank containing a mature bull because just their presence may serve to irritate him.

The conflict aroused by a confrontation between two equally matched young adult males must be tremendous and the results can be ludicrous. Their prior experiences have taught them that the encounter offers a potential source of constant amusement or social interaction. On the other hand, increasing testosterone levels (hormone levels regulating sex characteristics) along with the concurrent development of territorial aggressiveness urge them to combat. Should they approach, withdraw, or fight?

Two such males housed in adjacent tanks with only a wire partition between them at Marineland of Florida spent most of their time threatening, posturing, and snapping their jaws at each other as long as each was safely on his side of the wire. However, when released together into a large adjacent swimming area, all hostility disappeared and they rushed toward each other like two old friends and spent their time in the communal tank enjoying fun and games together. The large tank apparently represented communal territory while the smaller holding tanks apparently were "home territory" to be defended at all costs.

Unless a female has a calf, she usually does not become very aggressive, but she may even kill a recently introduced animal if she has been permitted exclusive control over one area for several years.

Adults. Mature male adults range from 7½ to 8 feet in length to a reported 12 feet or more (mature females are slightly smaller). They eat about 12 to 15, or even 20, pounds of fish a day. The clean, slim bodies of young dolphins become heavier proportionately—but so gradually that one cannot say whether an individual is subadult or adult on that factor alone. This is judged more on body length and a change in behavior from the more active and playful animal to one that tends to show less undirected activity. This means, not that the animals become lethargic with maturity, but that they expend less overt effort exploring their environment. Adults remain alert, wary, and ready to use their powerful muscles very quickly if necessary.

Their muscular development and body control are extremely impressive. They make 16-foot leaps from relatively small tanks with sufficient accuracy to take a small fish from an attendant's mouth. Even higher leaps are well documented. Their swimming speeds require an expenditure of energy equivalent to that of the highly trained human athlete in prime condition. They can come to a dead stop or veer at the last possi-

This young adult female is just beginning to take on the heavier proportions typical of older dolphins. (Marineland of Florida)

The body control of dolphins is often amazing, as demonstrated by this female doing a somersault. (Marineland of Florida)

ble moment with almost perfect control. When so inclined, they can also precisely coordinate their swimming with other members of the community.

Adults give the appearance of sleeping more, but usually are roused to full alertness by the slightest change in their environment. Brain wave studies of sleep in dolphins offer fertile ground for investigators in this somewhat controversial field. It is often difficult to say for sure whether or not a dolphin is sleeping merely by looking at it, particularly when they slowly rise to breathe. Inasmuch as the very young appear to sleep, juveniles not to do so, and old adults to nap, the only way that this interesting question can be resolved is by such sophisticated studies. The question is not merely an academic one. In many ways the physiology of dolphins is similar to that of humans, and by studying the sleep patterns of the dolphins we may gain some insight into those of humans, especially in weightless space, which is akin to the almost weightless condition under which dolphins normally live.

This skull, from a large English adult, clearly shows the impressive array of conical teeth that all bottle-nosed dolphins have. (Marineland of Florida)

Mature animals do continue to play, although they do not spend full time at it as the juveniles appear to do. They tease a fish by coaxing it out of a hiding place with a piece of food and then grab the morsel away, or entice a person to play with them by proffering an object which they snatch away at the last split second as he reaches for it. We have had dolphins offer us bits of seaweed as well, much as a dog will do when it brings a stick to be thrown.

One male dolphin, a practical joker, learned a trick that wonderfully startled an unsuspecting human. A visitor from a local engineering company, ignoring the *Keep Out* signs around the animal's tank, went over to play with him. Although the rows of flashing teeth in a dolphin's mouth tend to make people unfamiliar with the animals a little jumpy at first, the encounter went well until the man tired of the games and began a conversation with someone nearby. While talking, he turned his back on the dolphin and leaned against the rim of the tank. The dolphin, however, was not ready to give up and rather sharply nudged the unsuspecting man in the back to remind him that they were supposed to be playing. The story goes that the man jumped at least 6 feet straight up in the air, yelled bloody murder, and took off running. When last seen, he was still going. No doubt this is somewhat exaggerated, but the reaction must have been impressive, because ever since that day this dolphin lives for the times he can catch other humans and pull the trick again. We sometimes let him play it on us just to make his day complete.

All dolphins seem to discover very quickly that humans react swiftly if water is squirted or splashed on them unexpectedly. The animals learn to go to great pains to give the appearance of lounging quietly and innocently in a tank with no thought of the passing humans — but let the inexperienced passer-by beware. Should he turn his back, he will likely get a healthy dose of cold water down his back.

By the same token, dolphins enjoy having people splash water at or on them, and the precocious one that we have mentioned several times especially likes to have a whole bucketful of water poured over his head as he sticks it up out of the water at tankside. Such games often develop as a result of normal daily activity. In this case, the dolphin's attendant would rinse his feeding bucket in the tank while his charge hovered nearby. One day the attendant poured the water over the dolphin's head and the game has continued almost daily ever since.

Dolphins play by themselves as well as with others. They toss dead fishes into the air and catch or go after them; they push toys around their tanks or endlessly carry inanimate or even animate objects about with them. They also devise games among themselves, passing back and forth pieces of fish or a piece of cloth that has fallen into the tank. Such objects may provide some form of competitive play for hours.

For example, a game was devised between a large adult female bottlenosed dolphin and a large male Risso's dolphin. As part of a show, the Risso's dolphin jumped for squid, his normal food. However, at the end of his act, and in order to lure him from the feeding platform when it was time for another dolphin to jump, a large firm-bodied fish was included with the last handful of squid. He swallowed the squid but retained the fish in his mouth and swam with it around the tank while the large bottlenosed dolphin followed The game consisted of his trying to entice her to take the fish from his mouth. If she failed to come close enough, he then let it float away. When she approached, he would pick it up again or, if it was hanging far out of his mouth, suck it back in so that she could not get it. The bottlenosed dolphin obviously considered it a game too, for she rarely made a rush for the fish and seemed not to

Adults also play. Here an old female balances a bit of rag on her flipper. (David K. Caldwell)

This female made a regular game of pushing this small sea turtle around and around her tank. (Marineland of Florida)

want to get it for a while either. Sometimes she appeared deliberately to act uninterested, thus decoying him into dropping it. After five or ten minutes the two would tire of their game, and the Risso's dolphin would allow the bottlenosed dolphin to take the fish. This performance went on at each of six daily shows for several weeks.

Some visitors to oceanariums insist on tossing shiny coins into the dolphin tank, despite the pleas of the attendants. These coins are often seized upon as play items, and a dolphin may spend hours carrying the coin in its mouth to the surface, dropping it, and following it down to catch it again just before it hits the bottom. Unfortunately, the tendency of the dolphin is to swallow the coin when he tires of the game, and this can cause problems and even death due to intestinal blockage. We once found nearly a dollar in pennies in the stomach of a dolphin that died in captivity. The coins were of recent date and probably the brightest the visitor had to offer. When two or more animals play with an object, the problem is compounded because there is an even greater chance that one of the dolphins will swallow it rather than let its opponent have it.

Despite the inclination to play with almost anything, it generally is something familiar, for dolphins usually flee from any strange object that enters their environment. It is inspected from afar, and approached slowly, with caution. Early approaches are accompanied by much echolocation and visual attention; readiness for a quick retreat is revealed in the dolphin's body posture. Even when another animal is being put into a community tank, the residents herd together as far away as possible and turn and face the gate where the new animal is entering. Once it is in the tank, the resident dolphins swim over to investigate the newcomer by means of echolocation and visual inspection; special attention sometimes involving touch with the tip of the snout is usually given to the genital region.

A new diver or a diver doing a new job also receives careful attention, probably because he is another kind of animal invading the community, even though on first glance he looks the same as the experienced diver

This dolphin has overcome any fear that it might have had of these Florida brown pelicans and they must now beware their tail feathers. (Marineland of Florida)

doing a familiar job. A new diver tends to be unsure of himself and somewhat afraid of these large sleek dolphins swimming around in their tank, which he is entering for the first time. The dolphins seem to sense this, and their own natural fear is apparently replaced by their strong desire to tease. The new man, therefore, sometimes receives harmless but merciless buffeting by the playful dolphins. A trained diver who acts afraid receives the same buffeting, but as soon as he regains his self-confidence the dolphins quickly lose interest and go on their way, showing that it is the unusual behavior that attracts their attention and not a man in a familiar diving suit.

The dolphins' fearful reaction to strangeness in the environment is a quality believed to go along with advanced intelligence. While many mammals are alert to strange things around them, they often do not show an inclination to flee unless the new thing is another animal that appears likely to attack. Although dolphins adapt well to captivity, they

49

often do not readily accept new situations in that environment. For example, when an object that is to be used as part of a new show is placed in a tank of dolphins, it will often produce first silence and immobility and then a frenzy of loud vocalizations and panic to avoid it. To help them overcome their fear, the object is continually introduced and removed or is allowed to float in the tank away from the dolphins. Often they will hurriedly try to toss it out of the tank, much as a human might try to kick away a scorpion even though it represents danger and revulsion. The desire by both dolphin and man to get rid of an offending object overcomes the normal fear of it, especially when the shared space is cramped. New dolphins rarely evoke this much fear, nor does putting an animal into a different tank. It is a foreign object—a ball or a piece of equipment or even a piece of string—that throws the dolphins into a state of fear that sometimes lasts for several days.

Since dolphins almost always avoid unpleasant situations by moving as far away as possible, it was surprising to note on one occasion the opposite behavior by an adult female that had been captive for a number of years. She was sick and needed injections of antibiotics twice daily, so she had to be run into a shallow receiving area where the attendants could

Each new arrival is given a careful inspection by the residents. (Marineland of Florida)

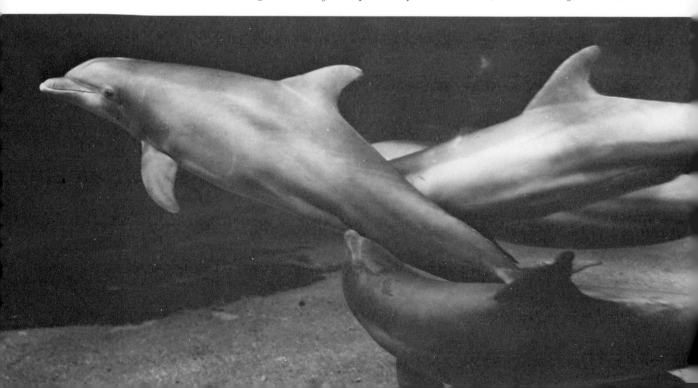

Sick or not, this female puts all 300 pounds into forcing her tank gate closed in order to avoid coming out for an injection of antibiotic. (Marineland of Florida)

reach and hold her easily. The area chosen was familiar to her: it was the flume between her holding tank and the large show tank where, as part of her daily show routine, she waited, enclosed between two gates, until it was time for her act. It took only a short time for her to decide that the flume was an undesirable place and that if she stayed in her own deep holding tank she could not be given the shots. However, instead of retreating to the side of the tank farthest from the gate, which was the expected behavior, she began to push against the holding tank gate to prevent its being opened, even coming partly out of the water to lean against it. A 300-pound-plus dolphin is a strong animal even when sick, and the attendants had to apply considerable force to open the gate and keep it open. Even when they managed to open it partly, the dolphin would come around behind and close it again. To understand the problem and solve it in that direct manner instead of retreating is noteworthy, and indicates a level of reasoning not usually found in animals when danger is involved.

51

Pre-mating behavior often involves violent head bumping. (David K. Caldwell)

The dolphin female is thought to become sexually mature at six to eight years of age. She frequently takes the lead in courtship. She may attempt to entice a male by rubbing against him, presenting her underside to him, or inserting the snout or tip of the fluke or flipper into his genital slit. A female in captivity frequently positions herself so that the fluke, flipper, or dorsal fin tip of a male is inserted into her own genital aperture. Once the male is stimulated, courtship often develops into what appears to be a violent fight in which they bump heads forcefully.

52

The two animals swim straight toward one another, head on, until they either hit full force (the area of impact is well padded with fatty tissue) or glance off and slip down each other's side. Intromission is rapid and takes place underwater almost belly to belly, with the male coming up from underneath at an angle.

Except in captivity, where opportunities for mating are greater, males are not effectively sexually mature until they are about twelve years old. The older males, or bulls, are in complete command of a group and need only to face a young male or even a female of any age to exert their dominance. Often they are quite aggressive, and in captivity have been known to butt forcefully and even kill young animals that tried to challenge them actively or that offended them simply by their presence. Large males take no part in rearing the young, but do tolerate their play and, in their role of providing protection for the herd as a whole, actively defend them along with the females. These older males are most likely the ones that impregnate females in the wild. Normally, the young ones, which do produce a few sperm, know how to copulate, and are physically capable of it if given the opportunity that they have in captivity, do not have the chance to mate with females unless a large bull is absent. This situation has led to some misinterpretation regarding age of maturity. It is one thing to be sufficiently sexually mature physiologically to produce a few sperm and quite another to be sufficiently sexually mature behaviorally to defend and maintain a harem and thus father the young.

Strong bonds of affection between individuals in captivity are well known. Not only do two animals prefer to associate more with each other than with others in the same captive colony, but these relationships are often retained for long periods of time even when the animals are separated. There have been cases of two dolphins being separated for a number of months and then returned to each other's company. From their behavior it was obvious that they recognized each other and that their old bonds were quickly re-established, regardless of what new social ties had been developed in the interim.

Old Age. Preliminary results in studying the ages of dolphins by their teeth (similar to the way the rings in tree trunks are used to age the tree) suggest that dolphins reach an age of at least twenty-five years, and probably more. We know of one captive animal at Marineland of Florida that lived to the age of twenty-one (she was born there) before dying of a malady other than old age. Another animal still living there at this writing was born there eighteen years ago.

Our data on old age are slight, but we believe that the very old animals are not sexually active, tending to regress in fertility as they grow older. What role if any these older animals play is not known, although the females may sometimes be the aunties.

The color of the older adults stays about the same, except that the older females may develop an inconspicuous spotting along the sides and on the belly. On autopsy, such animals always show evidence in their ovaries of having borne young, while ones that lack the spotting (sometimes only one or two spots may be present) in our experience generally do not. The spotting, therefore, apparently is a secondary sexual characteristic. We rarely find this spotting on males, even fully adult ones, and when we do it is on extremely large animals. We have also seen several very large females that had an entirely gray belly (except for almost-white coloring around the umbilical scar and the genital region), but do not know if this was the result of advanced age or lifetime pigmentation. We rarely see this gray belly pigmentation on males, but again it is only on very large individuals. We have not seen such gray undersides on young animals. We have also seen several old females that appeared grizzled around the eyes and blowhole. Again, we do not know whether this was a sign of old age—as it often is in terrestrial mammals—or the lifelong pigmentation of the individual. Older animals, by the nature of their play, fight, and sexual activities, and sometimes through circumstances of their environment such as disease and contact with sharks, also tend to have more scars and other disfigurations than the young animals. However, inasmuch as such scars appear to remain with the animal for life, it is difficult to say when they were put there.

Dolphins in the Wild

THE SEAS, inland waterways, and bays so commonly frequented by bottle-nosed dolphins are extensive, and the inshore waters in which most seem to live are usually turbid. Those that live farther out at sea and in clearer waters are not often easy to find. In addition, observations of behavior in the wild are limited because wild dolphins are skittish, except when swimming in, or "bow riding" (making use of the forward pressure of the wave as it is pushed up by a moving vessel) the bow wave of ships, or under rare and unusual circumstances that will be discussed later in this chapter.

An early view of Marineland of Florida (circa 1939), where dolphins were first success-fully bred in captivity. Typical wild dolphin habitats surround the oceanarium, from open ocean beach in front to the marshes and waterways behind. (Marineland of Florida)

Many of us have seen certain types of behavior such as the bow riding, but there are other types that hardly anyone has seen, or at least reported, and many more that have never been reported in the wild, although from observations of captive dolphins we are sure that they must occur. The previously detailed similarities between the few observations of behavior in the wild and the much more extensive and detailed reports of behavior in captivity are gratifying to those of us who study the captive animals. We have some degree of confidence that we can relate most of the behavior of these dolphins to normal behavior in the wild.

Additional information about the biology of the species has been obtained by careful study of dead animals washed ashore or from the few dolphin fisheries scattered around the world. By piecing together bits of information from each of these sources, and corroborating the findings where data from several sources overlap, much can be learned of the biology of the bottlenosed dolphin or other similar species.

Social Organization. Although the size of herds of some kinds of dolphins may exceed several thousand, we have never heard of herds of bottlenosed dolphins that numbered more than a few hundred, and that size is rare. Most bottlenosed dolphins are seen in groups of a dozen or less; the largest may consist of perhaps fifty to a hundred or so individuals. When a larger herd appears, it seems to be scattered over a wide area and is broken up into very small groups of no more than a dozen individuals (and usually only three or four). We know only a little of the sexual composition of these groups, but what we do know suggests that they have definite forms and that they are not random individuals swimming together in the same area.

The small groups of which we have knowledge are believed to consist of several adult females and their offspring (up to two years of age), with a large adult male and several subadult males and females nearby. Others appear to consist of groups of juveniles that may or may not be sexually segregated. From limited data based on captures of entire small groups (or "pods") of juveniles, it seems to be the general rule that the sexes are segregated in each pod, although there are exceptions to this. Several of these pods of either family groups or groups of juveniles go to make up a larger herd. The pods have been observed to come close to one another, and even swim through one another for a few minutes; but whether or not there is intermixing between them has still to be determined. Nevin Stewart, a dolphin catcher working the northeastern Gulf of Mexico, who has observed such encounters between pods from the air, does not believe that they intermix permanently. Sexually segregated pods are not limited to the juveniles, for recently we learned of a pod of five large animals, considered to be of adult size, all of which were males.

In time of danger, as during a capture when a net is surrounding a large school, dolphin "scouts" appear to examine the situation and sometimes to take such direct action that they are in considerable danger. In our experience, the largest male did not do the scouting, as one might expect; one of the subadult males did. The subadult male is biologically expendable to the herd, being lower in the social hierarchy than the herd bull and less likely to impregnate the females. Thus by acting as scouts,

A wild dolphin heads away from the boat to scout the shrinking circle of net. (Aquatarium)

the subadult males help protect the herd without endangering its long-term social structure or reproductive potential, and thus help maintain the species. In the event that the pod does not contain subadult males, any one of the larger animals of the group—male or female, subadult or adult—appears to assume the role of charger. It takes little to open an avenue of escape for a herd of dolphins, and once the top of the net is lowered, the bottom lifted, or a hole opened, the rest of the herd charges through to freedom. The encircled dolphins rarely jump a net, although this is not unknown during attempts at capture. If they do not escape as a consequence of charging it, they usually are captured.

One of the most appealing traits dolphins exhibit is that they render aid to members in physical distress. An examination of old whaling literature reveals many reports of several species of whales and dolphins having aided one of their kind. In géneral, assistance takes two forms: one, known as "standing by," involves the herd members merely staying close to an injured or restrained member. The other involves actual physical support of an injured individual at the surface by one or more herd members—an action that prevents the distressed animal from drowning, even if it means possible injury or death to the remaining uninjured animals.

A new mother tries to lift her stillborn calf to the surface. Her wide eyes denote her extreme excitement. (Marineland of Florida)

Bottlenosed dolphins give assistance to others in several ways, both in captivity and in the wild, and it was in this species that actual physical support was first clearly demonstrated when one animal was accidentally knocked unconscious while being transferred into a pen at Florida's Gulfarium. Two other members of its herd immediately began to support the stunned animal at the surface until it recovered. One dolphin on each side placed its head under a flipper of the injured dolphin in order to hold it at the surface. Similar support has since been seen in the wild.

A series of experiments designed to see what might elicit this behavior, combined with an evaluation of reports in the existing literature on assistance either in the wild or in captivity, suggests that such behavior is widespread among the cetaceans but that it does not occur each time circumstances would seem to warrant it. There are always exceptions to any behavioral observations, but it appears that usually only young of either sex or adult females are aided. Adult males do not commonly receive help. This generalization holds for both standing by and direct support. It is also much more likely that support will be given to an animal familiar to the group than to a stranger—even if the criteria of proper age and sex are met. Individuals of either sex may do the supporting or standing by, but females seem more likely to do it when there are enough animals so that one or two may volunteer. This particular behavior may be related to, but is not the same as, maternal defense of the young or maternal aid to a young one needing help.

Either standing by or support is not restricted to other individuals of the same species. Dolphins of different species, especially when they have been tank mates for a long time, may aid one another when in distress, and bottlenosed dolphins have been involved in such aid. Such interspecific assistance has also been reported in the wild.

Despite some controversy, we do not believe that wild dolphins would be likely to support humans, such as downed fliers. We feel that a flier would be too strange an object for the dolphins. Even if there should

A mother and her young calf. (Marineland of Florida)

be a well-documented report by a careful and unbiased observer in which a dolphin pushed a human to shore, there are probably just as many examples of a dolphin pushing a person farther away from land, to be lost forever as a possible source of information.

We have found by using models or stillborn young, that instead of supporting a strange body, a confined dolphin is more likely to try to defend its territory against the intruder. This does sometimes take the form of pushing—but the pushing is to rid the area of the body, not to offer support. If in being shoved away the body is pushed into shallow water (that is, "to shore"), a human observer might have reason to think the dolphin is making a purposeful attempt to save that body. Dolphins show no evidence of supporting even a strange dead dolphin, so why should they support such a totally strange animal as a human? There is every reason to expect, however, that dolphins could be trained to support and defend humans in the water since these actions are already part of their normal behavior.

We have seen supportive behavior and can vouch for it. However, it seems to us that much more is involved than a reflex action—one dolphin may even try to prevent another from injuring itself. We have

60

seen preventive behavior once, and have had it reported to us on two other occasions by qualified observers working at other places.

In our personal observation, a mother kept her year-old distressed female infant from bumping into the tank wall by forcing her snout between the struggling infant and the wall. This behavior continued for an hour or two before the calf died. An adult female reportedly did the same thing for another adult female. The aided female apparently lost her ability or desire to echolocate as a consequence of a terminal illness, and the other dolphin (herself sick) directed the seriously ill animal into a normal circular swimming pattern whenever she began to bump into the tank wall. When the dying dolphin was swimming normally, the aiding animal left her and resumed her own swimming pattern. This intermittent aiding continued until the sick animal died several days later.

In the third example, a juvenile male actively prevented a newly introduced injured tank mate from bumping into the tank wall for a day or more. It was reported that he continued his action without interruption until the injured animal died. Since the death occurred at night, we do not know if it resulted from failure of the assisting dolphin to keep up its behavior, or if the assisting dolphin ceased his efforts because the other animal died.

We have been told by dolphin collectors (fishermen who capture dolphins for exhibition and study) that the mothers of young will often position themselves between a boat and the calves, and that if a calf ventures too close to the boat or net on its own, the mother will force it away by coming between it and the strange, dangerous object.

Calving. Our observations of the schools of wild dolphins in northeast Florida suggest that most calves are born in the spring or summer. Some few newborn infants are seen in the same schools all year round though, and this birthing pattern coincides with those in captivity in the same area at Marineland of Florida; that is, a few calves are born each season of the year, but most are born in the spring and early summer.

As usual, things are not as simple as this would seem to indicate, for in the southern part of the same state more calves are born in mid- and late summer. Dolphins taken from northeastern Florida to California change the time of calving to fall, which suggests that seasonal differences are due to some environmental factor or factors rather than to a genetic characteristic. As yet we do not understand what causes such variations in calving season, but they may be related to water temperature or intensity and duration of light. As the females seem to be sexually receptive during a large part of the year, the variation in season of birth and consequently in time of impregnation may be related to reproductive variation in the males.

Habitat and Range. We have mentioned briefly some of the major habitats in which bottlenosed dolphins may be found. Again, these include the waters along the open ocean beach extending seaward perhaps some 50 to 100 miles, but usually much less, and the protected waters of the ocean inlets, bays and waterways, and marshes. The depths may range out to the edge of the continental shelf, or to some 100 fathoms (600 feet), but for the most part dolphins appear to live in waters not much deeper than a few hundred feet at most. This is quite different from some of their more offshore cousins. Even bottlenosed dolphins that happen to live in some geographical locality where deep oceanic waters come close to shore—as around some of the West Indian islands and the Pacific coast of North America—are most often close to land. Thus bottlenosed dolphins can be said to be an inshore species at almost all times and a shallow-water species when physical factors, such as depth of coastal waters or presence of bays and inlets, permit.

Available evidence suggests that bottlenosed dolphins do not make the long migrations characteristic of certain species of the large whales. However, there does seem to be reason to believe that those living close inshore make two types of short migration between restricted home

Each spring the nearly extinct black right whale migrates north along the Florida coast from some unknown calving ground. Bottlenosed dolphins often accompany them for hours at a time as the whales proceed on their slow journey. (Wometco Miami Seaquarium)

ranges. The first migratory pattern is up and down and is limited to a probable distance of 50 to 100 miles. The second is a limited invasion of the bays and rivers. The first is back and forth along the coast and postulated as influenced by the sun; the second is up and down protected waterways and is postulated as being under tidal influence. Additionally, there appear to be two kinds of predictable daily movements, which are much more limited in distance and time.

Carolina Snowball, a true albino female. (Wometco Miami Seaquarium)

Dolphins with peculiar colorations or characteristic scars or other injuries provide us with additional information, for they have natural tags. Man-made tags, in the form of colored disks or streamers, or even radios, must be attached to dolphins and traced before we can make positive statements, but we believe from these naturally marked animals that dolphins have a relatively restricted home range. We have no information as to how far seaward this home range might extend. There is also reason to believe that this might more correctly be recorded as the dolphin's having a very restricted home range of only some 10 miles or so, a traveling range to another spot, and then another restricted home range on the other end, somewhat like a dumbbell in over-all shape.

The record of one of the more famous dolphins, Carolina Snowball, a full albino once held by the Wometco Miami Seaquarium, suggests this. Before she was captured for exhibit, she lived in a very restricted region off the coast of South Carolina and became so well known there that she was almost a local treasure. She would live in one locale for weeks at a time, and was seen by local fishermen nearly every day. There were also reports of a white dolphin in Georgia waters, and this animal, too, reportedly remained in one area for long periods. However, each dolphin disappeared for several weeks, only to return again.

This indicates that Carolina Snowball lived for a few weeks in one restricted home range, moved to the second restricted home range rather rapidly, and stayed there for a while before going back to the first one. Records of sightings are not precise enough to say definitely that a white dolphin was never in both localities at the same time; however, when the white dolphin from South Carolina was captured, the one from Georgia ceased to appear, further indicating that it was the same animal.

We know of other unusually colored dolphins that have followed a similar pattern off the west coast of Florida and off the mouth of the Mississippi River. We have also seen unusually scarred individuals maintain a home range of only a few miles' diameter for over a year, and have heard of others that stayed in one locality for almost three years. These animals were in no way restricted; nor were they encouraged by humans (feeding them, for example) to stay in one region.

Not only are individual dolphins limited in their geographical ranges (a matter of miles) or habitats within that range, but they also demonstrate a tendency to hold to a very restricted area within each habitat. People who study dolphins closely in the wild because it is their business to catch them tell us that a particular group of dolphins is always found within the bay, while another group may always be found along a certain stretch of ocean beach just off the bay or near a certain buoy offshore. The distances between the different habitats (sometimes called microterritories) could sometimes be measured in yards, not miles; yet there is good reason to believe that the individual dolphins stick to their microterritories when occupying that particular geographical home range and only rarely venture from it.

Microterritories also exist in dolphin community tanks, as our own observations have revealed. When space permits, a dolphin will have a preferred spot where most of its resting time is spent. At active times, the dolphins tend to enter each other's microterritories; but when there is no special activity like feeding or play going on, each dolphin takes

Young spotted dolphins, like the one shown here with an adult, are often mistaken for bottlenosed dolphins. Their similarity in color probably accounts for reports of mixed schools of the two species. (David K. Caldwell)

its place and often defends it from an intruder by a chase, jaw clap, open-mouthed gesture, or just a stare. Preferred places seem to be near the surface at the center of the tank or near a jet of incoming water. A spot near the surface would be advantageous for breathing. Since dolphins seem to enjoy having water flow over them, a place near a stream of incoming water would seem to be a sensuously desirable one. They often place their snouts in the flow or even into the pipe opening itself.

Captive dolphins are also sometimes maintained in small holding tanks or in small pens directly connected to a larger tank in which they perform. Some individuals defend these small living areas with special vigor, even though the tanks are usually large enough to hold several animals without their being cramped. The defense varies from mild and short-lived chases to vigorous biting and even killing the intruder. Our own special research dolphin was the victim of a night in the tank of an established animal, and though his cuts soon healed, he will bear the scars for life. In another case we are told that an established adult female bottlenosed dolphin once killed an adult female spotted dolphin that was placed in her holding pen. Unlike our juvenile male, which had just come in from the wild and been placed with another recently captured but established juvenile male, the adult spotted dolphin was also well established in captivity. This over-all behavior, then, is one that those of us who keep dolphins must always consider when animals are rearranged for various reasons.

Underwater observations by William E. Evans in California have shown that wild herds tend to maintain such microterritories within the water column (a segment of water extending from surface to bottom). As in the case of the captive animals, it would be more desirable for breathing to be near the top of the water column close to the surface rather than down low in the column, where a dolphin not only would have to swim farther for air but might also have to come in some sort of physical conflict with individuals in the column above. The more dominant animals would be expected to position themselves closest to the surface. This is obvious in a tank, which has a limited surface, and interesting that it should occur in the wild where the amount of surface generally would not be thought to be a limiting factor. Why the animals persist in living in different depth layers in the water instead of spreading out in a single layer near the surface is not yet understood.

The second kind of short migration bottlenosed dolphins probably make is into bays and into rivers, and dolphins with peeling skin, trailing barnacles, and firmly clinging lice provide us with additional information about distribution in the wild. For although they cannot be considered a fresh-water species, they do sometimes move into fresh water and stay there for a few weeks. In Florida, they come up the St. Johns River as far as the city of Palatka, but even though the water up to that point (some 75 miles from the river's mouth) is fresh by human standards, it is somewhat unique among fresh waters in allowing marine animals to penetrate it deeply due to the large amounts of calcium chloride. This does not make it taste or feel salty, as does the sodium chloride of the ocean; however, it serves many of the physiological needs of the marine, or salt-water, fishes and crabs penetrating it.

67

Wild dolphins often share their more protected habitats with the Florida manatee, or sea cow. (Marineland of Florida)

Many, often huge, springs bubble up through the great limestone deposits upon which Florida rests, and calcium is released in the process. These springs feed into the St. Johns and other Florida rivers, up which the dolphins sometimes come. Although they seem to restrict themselves to the large rivers where there is still some tidal influence, some of the fresh-water bays that dolphins occasionally enter are not of the proper salinity, however, and their skin may be sufficiently affected to begin to peel. Since this does not happen overnight, it suggests that dolphins may spend as long as several weeks living in such seemingly unsuitable habitats without other harm.

In speaking of local bottlenosed dolphins in northeastern Florida, experienced collectors believe that some spend most of their time in the open sea while others live primarily in the protected salt "rivers" (waterways) and marsh streams. The men refer to these two groups as "ocean porpoises" and "river porpoises." Although we have not marked dolphins in this region, it has been our experience that a large percentage of those collected in the open ocean are infested with a conspicuous, fleshy, purplish barnacle that is found only on cetaceans; whereas those collected in protected waters almost never are. These barnacles, which are usually attached to the tips of the dorsal fin and flippers and the rear edges of the tail flukes, are so obvious that it is easy to see them on dolphins as they swim in the wild—it is not even necessary to capture an animal to see whether or not it is carrying the barnacles. The barnacles seem to act as identification marks that bear out the beliefs of the fishermen regarding ocean and river dolphins.

Although we have fewer data on another external parasite, a small crustacean whale louse, the record seems to substantiate the difference in dolphin distribution. Although the lice are found less frequently than the barnacles, only dolphins captured in the open ocean have borne them.

The higher salinity in the open sea may be a prime factor in this different distribution of external parasites, and while there is almost surely an interchange of dolphins between river and ocean, the animals have to remain in one major habitat or the other for long periods of time in order for the lice and barnacles to become attached and grow or be lost without fragmentary remains (the basal shell, in the case of the barnacles) still attached to their hosts.

There is reason to believe from frequent observations along the beach that a daily alongshore movement in a limited sense may take place. Scientists feel that the observed daily movements of common dolphins in the western Mediterranean are related to the position of the sun, with the animals heading east into the rising sun and west into the setting sun. Local movement of dolphins along the northeastern coast of Florida appears to be southeasterly in the morning and northwesterly in the afternoon, closely following the coastline. Inasmuch as the sun circles through the southern sky they seem to be swimming toward the sun at all times.

If indeed dolphins of any species tend to travel back and forth over roughly the same course for a generally fixed number of miles in one day, this would tend to keep them in one somewhat restricted geographical region. It might in part account for their slight daily or seasonal variations in appearance at a given spot, since such factors as cloudiness, currents, wind drift, or even feeding would affect movements in such a way that the central point of the daily movement would shift from day to day and season to season.

There is also evidence that dolphins may be influenced in their daily local movements by the tides. The ones that live in the inland waterway near St. Augustine appear to move south of the city some 15 to 25 miles during a falling tide, remain in a certain general area during the low tide, and then move back north beyond the city on the highest part of the tide, returning south when the tide begins to fall. These movements in inside waters deserve considerably more study; but a few observations by us and many more by long-experienced fishermen suggest that they occur, whatever the causative factors may be.

There is still much to be learned about dolphin migrations, but we do know that the numbers of animals in an area seem to vary from time to time during the day and from season to season. Where they go when they are not seen is unclear. The large schools or herds sometimes seen in northeastern Florida waters in spring and early summer may only be the result of a concentration—for some yet uncertain reason—of the many small and widely scattered family groups or individuals that are present in the general region most of the year. On the other hand, during the months of September and October, almost no dolphins are seen in the area, and we can only conclude that some longer movement, either alongshore or offshore, is made.

A population of very large bottlenosed dolphins seems to exist farther offshore Florida than the range of most of the individuals of this species, but there is no proof of an inshore-offshore migration (either seasonal or daily) of bottlenosed dolphins as there is for their close relatives, the spotted dolphins. That species occupies much the same range in mainland waters of the western North Atlantic.

We have never seen, nor have we heard of, a mass stranding of bottlenosed dolphins, although there are such strandings in other dolphin species. Two or three bottlenosed dolphins on the beach at one time are the maximum we have heard about, and the cause of death of at least some of them is known. A live bottlenosed dolphin on the beach is extremely unusual. Death of individuals, as with most solitary strandings in our experience, is most likely due to injury or disease. The lack of mass strandings may be related to the fact that one of the major habitats of bottlenosed dolphins is just off the beach. The area is so familiar that there is less likelihood of mass stranding from panic or some similar cause.

Food and Feeding. Bottlenosed dolphins are primarily fish eaters, although they do sometimes eat a small amount of squid and a few shrimp. Because dolphins occasionally feed on shrimp, commercial fishermen sometimes consider them a nuisance and kill them. There are now laws that theoretically protect dolphins from any kind of persecution, and rightly so. Rather than living off shrimp, or any fish species of great commercial value, dolphins apparently eat mostly those fishes that in the industry are considered "trash" (commercially undesirable), and only rarely do they eat more than a few shrimp or commercially important fish at a time. Such so-called trash fishes appear to be forms that live in open waters, like needlefish and various members of the herring family;

Wild dolphins feed on leaping mullet in Matanzas Bay near St. Augustine, Florida. (Marineland of Florida)

Southern stargazer. Remains of these fish have been found in the stomachs of stranded dead dolphins. (Marineland of Florida)

those living near the bottom, like croakers and drum; and those burying into the bottom, like stargazers and eels.

It must be remembered that most fish have some commercial importance somewhere, and our statement that the dolphins do not eat fishes of commercial importance should not be taken absolutely literally.

Our findings from stomach contents of animals that have stranded after death so far provide no evidence that dolphins are major predators on commercial species. Although digestion is rapid, certain parts of the fish remain for a time in the first of the dolphin's four stomachs, and from even fragmentary remains, specialists can tell what the dolphin has been eating. Fortunately, such things as the hard beaks of squid can be identified as to species, as can the calcareous otoliths (or earbones) of fishes. Hard parts of other animals such as the horny carapaces of shrimp also can be classified to some extent, making the remains more valuable to the expert than one might think.

The size of the food doesn't seem to matter as long as the dolphin can swallow it, which it usually does whole. If a fish is too large, the dolphin may break it up by shaking it or by rubbing it along the bottom. At certain times of the year in the St. Augustine, Florida, area, for example, one may find large numbers of floating heads of sea catfish, neatly broken off by dolphins just behind the undesirable sharp projecting pectoral and dorsal spines of the fish. Fishermen commonly see dolphins doing this when the animals are feeding close to the beach or the fishing boats.

Dolphins often feed on the soft bodies of sea catfish after breaking off the head just behind the sharp spines of the dorsal and pectoral fins. (Marineland of Florida)

Even though individual dolphins apparently eat whatever kinds of small fishes they meet, they are also known to cooperate in catching fishes that school. They do so in several ways. First, one or more dolphins poke around in the soft bottom with their snouts and undoubtedly stir up fishes, which then become an easy catch for the other waiting dolphins. This might be termed "passive cooperative behavior," and probably results in the capture of such small fishes as grunts and small sea bass from around rocks, or small species of noncommercial soles. Active cooperative behavior also occurs when several dolphins chase fishes like small marsh minnows and yellowtail out of shallow marshy places or herd them against a shore.

The most striking cooperative action is when a group of dolphins find a large school of some pelagic fish species such as mullet or catfish and begin to encircle it from above, around, and below. The natural schooling behavior of such fishes is to keep in a tight ball, so the circling dolphins feed on the stragglers, or some dolphins charge through the school while others keep the ball intact. It is not known how long dolphins may herd a group of fish, but we have been told that they may do so for at least an hour.

Like many wild animals that have learned to live in the proximity of humans, dolphins have also learned to take advantage of certain human activities. In northeastern Florida, for example, they frequently follow shrimp boats, which drag large conical nets along the bottom, and apparently feed on the small fishes stirred up by the net. When the

73

A spotted dolphin joins its bottlenosed cousins at feeding time. (Marineland of Florida)

net is finally hauled in, the dolphins often gather closer around the boat to feed on trash fishes the fishermen throw back while sorting out the desired shrimp. It is interesting to note, however, that the dolphins do not necessarily take this free handout, for they have been seen feeding on catfish that they captured themselves while a fleet of shrimp boats worked nearby.

When feeding, wild dolphins rarely go into the frenzy that some animals do. Although there may be competition, especially in a confined tank, they seem to prefer dining in a leisurely way, and some of the dolphins appear to make a game of it by tossing fish into the air and dashing after them to catch them. This behavior is well known in captivity and has been observed in the wild as well. Wild feeding behavior is another area still to be studied in detail. Such a study should prove most interesting because the many types of fishes eaten must require a number of kinds of behavior on the part of the dolphins in order to make successful captures.

74

Some fishes absorb water directly through their bodies and do not need to drink, but dolphins do drink a certain amount of water. Most of their water is probably taken in by accident with their food, and still more is gained from the fishes that they eat. Like most mammals, they would sustain physiological harm if they drank too much salt water. Recent experiments in which dolphins were placed in tanks in water "tagged" with some trace element such as a minutely radioactive salt have shown that they do indeed drink small amounts, probably depending on the quality of their most recent food and on the amount of energy they have expended in swimming or other activity. Inasmuch as the dolphin has no sweat glands, water is probably retained in its body to a larger degree than in many mammals, and losses would occur chiefly through the normal function of the kidneys and in respiration.

Swimming. Unlike fishes, which have a tail oriented in the vertical plane and which, in general, they sweep from side to side while swimming, the tail (or flukes) of dolphins and other cetaceans is in the horizontal plane;

Streams of air bubbles issuing from the blowhole often accompany rapid swimming by whistling dolphins. (David K. Caldwell)

usually they swim by beating this up and down. The paired flippers are used both as stabilizing planes and sometimes as sweeps in propelling the animal in tight quarters; they may help steer on sharp turns and help brake on quick stops. As noted elsewhere, the dolphin uses its flippers to balance objects in play and to caress other animals socially. The dorsal fin also probably has some function in stabilizing the animal while it swims.

Unlike the flippers, which actually are modified arms, the dorsal fin and flukes are special evolutionary adaptations of the dolphin; they did not develop from a similar anatomical part in land mammals. There are still vestigial (remnant) bones remaining within the body of the dolphin (near the anal region) that once were the pelvis and legs of its land-dwelling ancestors, but these have no direct relationship to the flukes. The flukes have developed separately, contrary perhaps to outward appearances.

Much has been said in the more popular literature about the speed of swimming dolphins. Estimates vary up to some 50 miles an hour. Experimental studies have shown, however, that a maximum of about 18½ miles an hour is much more credible, and that even this is attained in bursts only. Prolonged swimming would have to be at a much slower rate, just as a human distance runner cannot maintain the speed that a sprinter might generate over a short distance. As one might expect, some kinds of dolphins are faster than others, and the bottlenosed dolphin probably is not one of the swiftest, although it can move quite rapidly for short runs.

Riding the bow wave of vessels has contributed to the controversy over the speed of dolphins, since they are able to go as fast as the ship when getting an assist from the bow wave, and can sustain this speed as long as they stay in the wave. At such times, hydrodynamic processes come into play, and if a dolphin positions itself properly, it benefits from the force created by the moving wave and has to exert little or no energy of its own. Experimental studies have suggested that the skin of

These dolphins line up in preparation for feeding time from a platform suspended high above the tank. (Marineland of Florida)

the dolphin is especially constructed so that it not only takes full advantage of hydrodynamic forces but also gives those forces an assist.

There is still much to do, however, before we have a full understanding of the reasons for the dolphin's excellent ability to move through the water with so little apparent effort. It is much like the bumblebee, which according to aerodynamic principles cannot fly but does so anyway. The dolphin's ability to attain fast speeds offers a fertile area for study. The information obtained from such studies could carry over to ship design and efficient use of energy by a scuba diver. Here again, as we enter the sea more and more, and begin to talk of it as a place to live and work in under certain needed conditions, the more we can learn from animals already living there the better.

Dolphins often swim in close and precise ranks, much like soldiers on parade. This is most obvious when seen from the surface as all of the animals come up as one to breathe, but it has also been observed below the surface of the sea. Dolphins in captivity also perform this close-order drill as they rapidly swim and leap in unison. Since such swimming

77

Dolphins often devise their own games. (Marineland of Florida)

is natural behavior, it is not too difficult to develop it into a show trick; but the animals must be carefully selected to work together—not all dolphins will perform in this manner. The greatest success is had with animals of similar size (age) and of the same sex. Even so, there are times when the members of the team squabble among themselves. On one occasion, we are told by Fred Lyons of Marineland of Florida, one of a performing trio began to lag behind in the unison jumps. Because this was a team effort, none of the dolphins received a fish reward. The trick was repeated several times, with two going unrewarded because their companion did not keep up. Finally, one of the two that had been doing his job turned on the offender and bit him several times on the head. After that, the offender kept up and all animals got their reward. No trouble has been reported since. These same individuals lived together or in adjacent tanks with a wire screen between and had been trained in the trick together from the start. Although a new animal could be worked into the routine, it would take considerable work on the part of the trainer to do so.

Diving and Respiration. Different species of dolphins have very different needs in diving, depending on their habitat and the kinds of food they seek. Some of the larger whales, such as the sperm whale, are known to dive as far down as half a mile and to stay down for as long as an hour. Bottlenosed dolphins, on the other hand, do not need to dive this far, since their normal habitat, except in certain geographical areas where deeper water is close to shore, rarely exceeds 100 feet or so. Frequently they are found in water barely deep enough for them to float. This is not to say that they are not capable of deep dives. Tuffy, the large male dolphin that has been used in Florida and California in cooperation with the Navy's Sealab programs, has been induced, through a series of fish-rewarded steps over a long period of time, to dive to a depth of some 1,000 feet. We hasten to add that it is difficult, if not impossible, to induce a large male dolphin to do anything at any time that he is not inclined to do.

During such a dive a dolphin holds its breath, and there is no need for decompression as it returns to the surface because the same volume of air is in its system when it comes up as when it went down. Decompression is required only when air is breathed under pressure, as by a deep-diving human scuba diver who takes fresh compressed air (or other gases) with him. This pressure must be relieved as the diver returns to the lesser pressure at the surface. In a deep dive the dolphin is limited only by the length of time that it can hold its breath.

Usually a dolphin breathes one or two times a minute when swimming in a normal manner at and near the surface. This rate may increase to five or six times a minute when it is swimming excitedly. On the other hand, a dolphin is able voluntarily to hold its breath for as long as seven minutes, and this permits deep diving or prolonged submergence, if circumstances should dictate it—for example, if it needed to swim a long distance underwater to escape some surface danger such as a pursuing boat.

There is evidence to suggest that a dolphin trained to do deep diving hyperventilates much like a human before a deep dive. Hyperventilation, or rapid series of breaths, increases the oxygen supply in the blood and helps drive out accumulated carbon dioxide. Even while breathing normally, a dolphin exchanges nearly all of the air in its lungs with each breath, leaving it with little residual stale air.

Although its physiology is such that a dolphin is able to retain more oxygen in its tissues than many mammals (which permits deep dives and concurrent long intervals between breaths), its normal oxygen requirements, as shown by experimentation, are probably similar to those of most land mammals. One aspect of diving physiology that is now under investigation in bottlenosed dolphins deals with the composition of the air in the dolphin's system after a deep dive. In this study, a dolphin has been trained to dive deeply and then to release a large bubble of air into a funnel leading to a collecting device before it fully surfaces. In this way a sample of air is obtained without its being contaminated by the air at the surface, and any changes in the composition of the sample as a result of the deep dive can be analyzed. Here again, the relative ease of training dolphins for such tasks, along with their similarity to humans in many body functions, permits the use of dolphins in experimental research that has human correlations.

Heat Exchange. Since dolphins lack sweat glands, they must rid themselves of excess body heat in some other manner. As long as they are in the water this poses no problem, for the water acts as a cooling agent. Out of water, it is quite a different matter, and when moving dolphins, human attendants must keep them wet or their internal body heat would soon cause them to die. This is probably the major cause of death of dolphins stranded on the beach.

Experiments have shown that the greatest transfer of heat away from the dolphin's body into the water is through its appendages—that is, its flippers, flukes, and dorsal fin. These are supplied with large blood vessels near their surface which act as carriers of heat, which is released

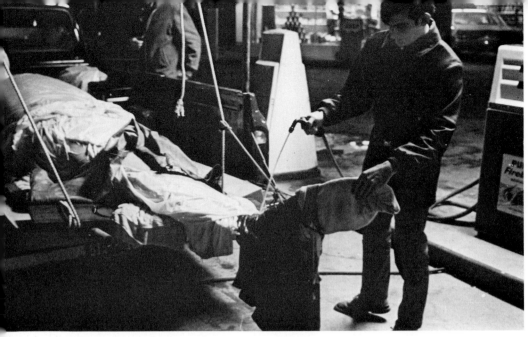

Dolphins and other cetaceans in transport must be kept wet and cool in order to avoid internal overheating. (Marineland of Florida)

and carried away by the cool water. This function of these appendages is obvious to anyone who touches a dolphin that has been out of water very long without having been kept properly wet. They feel almost red hot compared to the rest of the body—like a person running a terrifically high fever. If they are not cooled, the appendages eventually develop so much heat that they are permanently damaged, and may even be lost if the tissue is injured to the point that it dies and is sloughed off.

If a dolphin is in water that cannot circulate or is not cooled, its appendages also heat up to such a degree that damage can occur. Its body overheats, too, but not as obviously because it is protected by a thick layer of blubber. This layer not only helps insulate the animal against cold but also helps retain body heat when the animal is in cool water. Although internal damage could result, it is not as apparent as that which appears externally on the appendages, where most of the heat is concentrated and comes to the surface for discharge.

Play. Anyone spending much time watching dolphins in captivity is aware of the fact that they engage in considerable play. There also is good evidence that they play in the wild; probably bow-riding is the most obvious form.

81

Surf-riding in the wild is in many respects similar to bow riding and is probably to some degree the natural behavior from which bow riding developed after the advent of man and his ships. Living as they do close to shore, bottlenosed dolphins are usually the ones involved in such surfing behavior. While not commonly reported, dolphins indulge in it often enough for many people to have seen it. It happens in places where there is good surf on a sandy beach and where a regular population of dolphins is large enough to be in the area at times when the surf is up. It is obviously play, as there is no evidence that they are feeding or escaping some danger, for they continue surfing for as long as an hour in the same spot with no other apparent intent.

Observers stationed on a high dune or in a building near the shore have seen dolphins bobbing up and down in the swells out beyond the breakers awaiting a good wave much the way human surfers do. Also like the humans, the dolphins ride the crest and front of a wave and stay with it until the water is just deep enough to float them with ease.

On at least one occasion that we know of, near St. Augustine, a group of surfing dolphins was within sight of a group of human surfers, both catching the same big waves.

One of our captive dolphins, a juvenile male, sometimes makes his own waves by swimming (often upside down) around and around in his tank at a rapid pace until the water begins to slosh out in great sheets. With this motion to his satisfaction, he then stops swimming and bobs up and down in the series of waves that continue to course around the tank. He sometimes creates so much slosh that the water washes away the earth fill around his tank, and we must laboriously and frequently refill it. There is no doubt that this behavior is purposeful play.

A number of our associates who spend a lot of time fishing and boating in the waterways that wind through the marshes of northeastern Florida and southern Georgia tell us of seeing dolphins sliding out of the water onto the slippery wet mud banks that extend out from the marshes at low tide. Like surf-riding, this action is repeated many times by several animals together. Observers report that the animals often move well off into deep water before getting a fast swimming start for their slide, like children running on firm ground before a long slide on an icy sidewalk.

Sometimes a dolphin travels up a small tidal creek almost empty of water and then apparently chases a group of small fishes back into the deeper water where other dolphins lie in wait. At times the dolphin's movement up the small creek may cause a wave of water, containing fishes, to move along ahead of the large mammal. At the head of the creek, particularly on a mud flat, the water will not go any further, and begins to recede, leaving the fishes stranded long enough for the dolphin to eat them if it slides out onto the mud itself. Such behavior, apparently purposeful on the part of the dolphin, has been reported. In each case some sliding on mud is involved, since the water is often not really deep enough to permit the dolphin to swim. This unusual behavior is certainly related to the playful mud sliding, which possibly developed when some juveniles found it better sport than fishing.

A trusting dolphin will even leave the water for its trainer. (Marineland of the Pacific)

As with echelon swimming, sliding can be developed into a rather spectacular show trick in which a dolphin can be trained to come completely out of the water onto a platform. It may accomplish this by a belly slide forward or even a roll on its side; but no matter how it is achieved it is always most unexpected for an aquatic animal.

Activity Cycles. Whether or not dolphins sleep, and if so, how and how much, has been the subject of some disagreement. In our experience, we have found that old adults tend to doze near the surface a large part of the time. They sometimes even leave the blowhole out of the water so that they do not have to rise to breathe. Juveniles, on the other hand, seem to be able to go for prolonged periods without obviously sleeping. Using binoculars at a distance of several hundred yards, we observed a community tank of juveniles continuously for some thirty hours. We never saw them stop swimming and playing even to catnap.

Dolphins apparently do sleep a little, however, for we have come upon some that were still and quiet in the water but, when a slight sound was made, started as if being awakened. Whalemen have also reported this in the wild. Our own dolphin, passing from the juvenile to the subadult stage of life, sometimes floats at the surface on his back, with both flippers projecting into the air, and is so quiet and oblivious to nearby minor activity that we assume he is sleeping. He will continue this floating for several minutes if undisturbed, and will resume it immediately after a brief return to a normal belly-down position to blow. Even during this blow, in which he may take several breaths of air, he appears almost oblivious to outside activity and in either this blowing or belly-up floating position will appear surprised if the side of the tank is tapped. He is certainly not as alert as he usually is.

Also once, when we were recording sounds in a community tank, the dolphins went completely silent for a few minutes, although there was no danger to elicit such silence. They continued to swim in a circle, but their eyes were partly closed and they gave no evidence of doing more than keeping position. It is possible that some sort of half-sleep is sometimes involved, or "sleeping with the eyes open." The sounds uttered by adult dolphins emerging from a quiescent state are not typical. They are poorly defined acoustically, of lower frequency, and brief. Like humans, dolphins appear to require a few moments or even minutes to "get their voices awake."

Interaction with Humans. There have been rare instances in which wild dolphins have interacted closely with humans. One of the most famous is the New Zealand bottlenosed dolphin Opo, which permitted children to play with it in shallow water and even to ride upon its back. There have been other examples of this familiarity with humans that have not been so widely publicized. We know of no species of dolphin that has been involved in such incidents other than the bottlenosed. The closest thing to this behavior in another species involved a Risso's dolphin, by chance also from New Zealand. This individual, known as Pelorus Jack,* followed ships passing through Cook Strait, between the two large

---

*Editor's Note: The full and interesting story of "Pelorus Jack — A Dolphin Diplomat," by Cyrus Cress, was published in the May–June, 1955, issue of *Audubon Magazine.* It was later included in an anthology of animal stories entitled *The Audubon Book of True Nature Stories,* (1958), which may be referred to in public libraries. Antony Alpers also tells the story in great detail in his book, *Dolphins: The Myth and the Mammal* (1961).

85

Dolphins watch their cetacean cousin the grampus, or Risso's dolphin. (Marineland of Florida)

main islands that comprise New Zealand, and especially ones passing near the entrance to Pelorus Sound. The animal, of unknown sex, is said to have closely followed ships for over a quarter of a century, and because it became so famous there were special laws and regulations passed to protect it. Although this animal is said to have rubbed itself against moving ships, it did not come into direct physical contact with humans, as have wild bottlenosed dolphins whose inshore habitat makes such an association more likely.

One case in southeastern Florida involved a dolphin (called Georgy Girl) and children. In many ways this one was like Opo; it appeared and stayed in the area, allowing humans, especially children, to associate with it in the water. Other cases have been reported in Florida, but we do not have the documentation that is available for this one.

Despite the danger, a wild dolphin pushes aside a running outboard motor that appears to offend. (Florida's Gulfarium)

Perhaps a more unusual dolphin-human association in the wild is one that developed in northwestern Florida just west of Panama City when a dolphin of mature size came into a large bay during a storm. Crossing a sandy bar normally blocking the mouth of the bay except on the extra-high tides generated by the storm, it remained landlocked after the storm and took up residence in the vicinity of a fishing camp near the mouth of the bay. Since the bay extended for miles, the dolphin was not forced to select this spot, yet it voluntarily chose to do so, and soon began to permit swimmers to touch it and to play with it. While adults were allowed to play, this animal, like Opo and Georgy Girl, seemed to prefer the company of children, and would permit them much greater liberties in touching it than it did the adults—on the whole. It also developed another trait that became somewhat annoying to some of the local boatmen. It would swim up to running outboard motors and raise them out of the water with the tip of its snout or with the top of its head. We have heard many explanations for this behavior, including that the animal was seeking its mother and that the noise of the running motor attracted it. However, a running outboard motor sounds nothing like a living dolphin; in addition, this animal was too large to have been worrying about its mother. More likely it was annoyed by the sound—as remarked earlier, dolphins are often obviously annoyed with strange things in their environment. Captive dolphins give every indication that loud or high, whining noises are particularly disturbing—perhaps even painful—to them. Being somewhat tame from its other associations with humans, this one developed the courage to try to eliminate the disturbance from its daily life. On the other hand, it may have been simply a matter of play.

Off the coast of northeastern England and southeastern Scotland, another dolphin, an unusually large adult with a skin condition that made it readily identifiable, permitted scuba divers to associate with it in the open sea.

Undoubtedly, dolphin-human associations could develop often, provided a number of conditions were right. That they have happened since ancient times is suggested by the well-known "boy on a dolphin," so often depicted on early Greek coins and elsewhere in ancient art.

A number of experiments have been planned, using man and dolphin in cooperative underseas work; some have already been successfully

This wild dolphin allowed divers to swim with it in the open ocean near the English–Scottish border. The large size of the animal seems to be typical of adult European dolphins. (D. R. Smith, courtesy of G. R. Mundey)

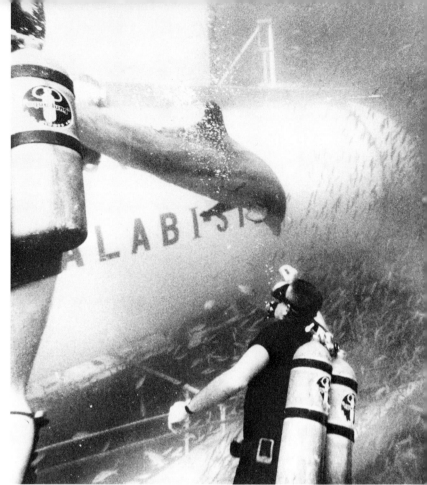

Free-swimming dolphin Tuffy works with divers in Sealab III practice at STEP (Submerged Technical Engineering Platform), formerly Sealab I, off Panama City, Florida. (Official U. S. Navy photograph)

tested in various pilot projects. The one with the most popular appeal involves the use of dolphins as free-swimming messengers and assistants in manned underwater habitat programs, the best known being the Navy Sealab project. In this program, dolphins have successfully acted as messengers, carrying mail or special tools to the habitat and then returning to the surface with something from below. We have already mentioned the deep-diving Tuffy. He has also served as messenger to Sealab habitats placed in much shallower depths, and he often carries his own packaged fish reward down with his other packages and receives it on the ocean floor from one of the human aquanauts working there.

One interesting part of this experiment has been the previously unknown reliability of the dolphin in open ocean work, in which it is perfectly free to swim away and never return if it so desires. Tuffy (as well as other dolphins) was trained to respond to a sonic recall signal, and he has never failed to do so. However, he once became the object of a major

89

air-sea search mission off California when a passing fisherman accidentally opened the gate of his floating pen and "let him free." Tuffy was probably totally confused by the situation when his usual routine was not available for him to follow, and he returned to his trainer only too willingly when he was finally found. It probably would have been difficult to determine which was the more relieved — Tuffy or his trainer.

In a recent similar situation, someone opened the pen of a dolphin being held at the Lerner Marine Laboratory at Bimini in the Bahamas. The animal refused to leave, and as the human who opened the gates was being led off by the local constabulary he was heard to mutter at the dolphin, "You have ruined me!" It is no kinder to release a captivity-oriented dolphin into a strange wild situation than it is to take someone's pet dog and release him in a strange forest. Such a dolphin is no longer a "wild animal" that must be pitied when penned up, and it is a disservice for a person, no matter how well meaning he may be, to release one.

In the past especially, when much less was known about dolphin behavior, oceanariums sometimes released dolphins for any of a number of reasons — lack of space or inability to learn required tricks. We know of two released dolphins that were recaptured under circumstances which suggested that the catch was not accidental and that the recaptured dolphins appeared to prefer the oceanarium to life in the wild.

In the first example, the dolphin was released by Marineland of Florida into the inland waterway nearby. Because there was no direct physical connection with the oceanarium tanks, the animal could not return to captivity on its own, and it remained in the area for some time before finally leaving. Some months later the Marineland collecting crew, while working in the general area near home, captured an animal (a bit too easily, they thought) that looked very familiar and acted as though it had been in captivity before. The original animal released there had not been marked and had no obvious scars to serve as natural tags; however, its general appearance convinced many of the personnel that it was the same dolphin, which had allowed itself to be captured again.

90

In the second example, the catchers working for the Aquatarium at St. Petersburg Beach, on the Gulf coast of Florida, brought in a dolphin that had a disfigurement. They later decided that it was not desirable to keep the animal for public appearances and it was released. It was soon recaptured, not once, but several times, and fishermen reported that the dolphin "almost seemed to chase them" whenever they came into view, in order that he might "jump into the net." At last report, he was back in the Aquatarium tanks.

We have one male dolphin that was taken from the wild when only a year or so old; he has been in captivity now for more than three years. One of our assistants, thinking that he would do the animal a favor by giving him a live mullet that had just been caught, tossed one into the dolphin's tank. The dolphin eagerly grabbed it in his mouth, the mullet gave one flap, and the dolphin dropped it like a hot potato. Unused to live fishes, he swam to the side of the tank farthest away from that thing that flapped and was so terrified that nothing could induce him to eat anything at all for twenty-four hours.

Possibilities for work a dolphin can perform in the open ocean might in the long run prove even more valuable and interesting than message-carrying to a fixed habitat. It is well known that search craft often have difficulty visually sighting a floating survivor, and airborne radio signals are often hard to receive even if batteries or other power sources are functioning properly. If a human survivor had some mechanical means of producing a specific underwater sound, a dolphin trained to that sonic signal could be released in the general area of the accident and could lead him to a submarine, habitat, or other specified place of safety. Potentially, it could also guide rescue ships to survivors if the location of a ship or air disaster were known. (Some of the television and other fictional writings about dolphins have used this kind of activity as a theme.)

Dolphins have already been used to locate missing inanimate objects by responding to a sonic signal or buoy that had been attached to it earlier when there was a possibility that it might be lost, as in the case of a piece of oceanographic sampling gear. It is much easier for a dolphin to carry out such a job than a human because the dolphin's acoustical system is so much better equipped to locate the direction of an underwater sonic signal. In addition, humans cannot begin to approach the dolphin's speed and mobility underwater.

We also believe that a dolphin might serve as a companion to a diver in a strange situation where unknown animate dangers, real or supposed, lurk nearby. We do not refer here to the suggestion that has been made that dolphins accompany divers to kill sharks or to patrol swimming beaches for sharks, both of which they might be trained to do. We think they could merely accompany a diver much like a dog on land that walks along a dark street with a human. The human feels more comfortable because the dog's senses are more attuned to things within the environment and can cover a large area. By the same token, a dolphin might at least make a diver feel more comfortable and less lonely even if it cannot cope directly with anything that threatened.

Dolphins versus Sharks. Aside from disease and internal parasites, dolphins would appear to have no major natural enemies other than sharks. The inroads man has made on dolphin populations are apparently next to

Dolphins and sharks do not always fight. (Wometco Miami Seaquarium)

A shark left its mark on this living dolphin but failed to get a meal. (David K. Caldwell)

insignificant, and dolphin losses through attacks by other predators such as killer whales (actually a large species of dolphin) probably are minimal since bottlenosed dolphins and killer whales (the most likely other predator) generally do not occupy the same ecological habitat.

There is a widespread popular belief that dolphins inevitably attack and kill every shark they see. This belief is especially prevalent among fishermen and others who spend a large amount of time around the sea. We recently joined in a study of this supposed phenomenon and have come to the conclusion that the interaction is not so simple and one-sided. Although dolphins undoubtedly do on occasion attack and kill sharks, they often apparently live together in some sort of harmony and in still other situations the dolphin unquestionably has come out second best.

We have talked to a number of fishermen who believe that they have seen dolphins attack sharks in the wild along the northeast coast and the west coast of Florida. Although we have not seen such an attack ourselves, the credibility of these observers is such that we have no reason to doubt them.

Because it is a somewhat controversial issue, with many people wanting to believe that the playful and friendly dolphin will always attack and kill the villain shark, we must point out that these same fishermen who have reported seeing dolphins attacking sharks have also told us that they have seen sharks attacking dolphins. Nevin Stewart tells us that he has seen dolphins in the northeastern Gulf of Mexico with fresh and still bleeding wounds which he believes were inflicted by sharks. One such wound involved the loss of an entire flipper. It is in the northeastern Gulf that we find so many dolphins with clear-cut, but healed, shark bites.

We have seen dolphin remains that have been removed from shark stomachs, and on one occasion we reached the scene just after a large shark had killed an equally large dolphin—an old and solitary female—and examined her mauled carcass. At that time we talked to fishermen who had observed the incident from a nearby fishing pier extending well out into the ocean, and all of them agreed that the shark had attacked her.

The number of dolphins that are captured with healed shark-bite scars is significant, and the shape of the scars with obvious shark tooth marks leaves no question that a shark caused the injury. Since dolphins carry scars for life, we cannot say when they receive them, but we tend to believe that the majority of shark bites are inflicted when dolphins are still young. We do not know how many young ones may be killed by sharks, but from our observations of captured animals many obviously survive. Young dolphins tend to be very inquisitive, and this coupled with the fact that their size makes them more vulnerable to attack leads us to make the assumption that they are the more common prey of sharks. The older animals that are attacked may be only those that are already weak from old age, disease, or injury—as was apparently true of the one old female that we saw.

We do have good evidence, however, that dolphins and sharks in the wild often live and even feed in the same area without apparent antagonistic interaction. In the St. Augustine region many dolphins and many sharks live close to shore. While we often see live dolphins bearing old shark-bite scars, we have never seen an attack by either on the other, or the known aftermath of one. Attacks by each have been reported locally, but only very rarely. From observers on the beach we also have reports of the two kinds of animals swimming in the same restricted area and apparently feeding together. Because sharks tend to get into a frenzy while feeding, it is quite possible that some of the scars we find on dolphins are the result of accidental shark blows during such a slashing frenzy when the two are feeding together in murky water on some common fish prey. While the clean bite marks on dolphins are probably the result of a direct shark attack, some of the slash-type scars may not be. Dolphins and sharks often have successfully shared a captive environment; they have also attacked one another in captivity. Owing to such unpredictable behavior, they usually are no longer displayed together, although in the earlier days of the business it was fairly common to do so.

As in most types of animal behavior, changing circumstances probably dictate whether or not dolphins attack sharks, sharks attack dolphins, or they live in harmony. A large shark, for instance, might attack a small dolphin when a small shark would not. There are records of a dolphin swallowing a small shark when obviously that same dolphin could not swallow a large shark. A healthy dolphin might not be attacked by a shark, whereas a sickly one probably would be. Dolphins in a group might attack a single shark, whereas a solitary animal probably would not, and certainly vice versa. The list of possible circumstances could go on for pages, but these examples should suffice to show that it is not a simple matter of which attacks which, but that a very complicated behavior pattern exists on the part of both dolphin and shark that deserves considerable additional study.

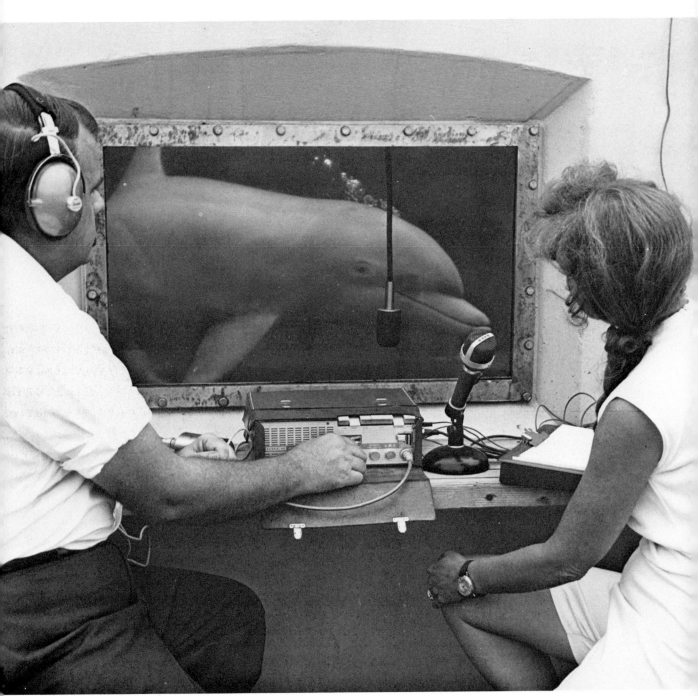

The authors at work recording dolphin sounds. (Marineland of Florida)

Sensory and Communication Processes

IF ANY WILD ANIMAL other than the dolphin were being discussed, the next few paragraphs would be unnecessary, for if we or other scientists speak of communication between protozoa, crabs, dogs, cats, or chimpanzees no thought is raised in the reader's mind as to the meaning. But the moment anyone learns that we are at present concentrating on dolphin communication processes, the person's prior exposure to unfortunately oriented publicity causes him to leap to the conclusion that we are studying dolphin language and that a complete dictionary of words will soon be available for purchase alongside the French-English and German-English dictionaries in the local bookshop. This is not so.

Results of dolphin communication studies have proved more interesting to us than the discovery of one more language, since we are zoologists and not linguists. We believe very deeply that mentally and emotionally we all have tended to place far too much emphasis on the verbal communication system of man, to the neglect of our more basic communicatory processes. These latter processes normally are learned at so young an age that we cannot remember that the learning took place.

Because these basic communication and learning processes are in many ways similar among all the advanced social mammals, it is worth while for us to study individuals of a species other than man that (1) will permit us to enter their home at any hour of the day or take up permanent residence among them if we so desire and (2) do not substantially

97

modify their behavior because of our presence. After displaying an initial curiosity, dolphins do not change their behavior just because an observer is present who might not approve of their natural conduct. In studies of dolphins and other nonhuman animals, communication does not mean or imply the use of words or even specific messages. In general, the longer and harder an investigator looks at animal messages, the more inclined he seems to become toward placing all signals into a single continuum of signals which indicate one of two things to another animal—either "stop" or "proceed."

Simplicity of message content does not mean that it is easy to understand. Social signals are sometimes not easy for us to understand, even in our own species. The animal itself is frequently in a state of conflict as to which it needs more, the company (stimulus) provided by another animal or the unoccupied territory (access to space, food, play, and sex objects) without the bother of competition. If the animal is in this state, the signals, which can and do arise solely as a result of the physiological state of the animal, of a certainty will be conflicting. Only in very clear-cut situations do dolphins give us unequivocal signals. From these we can work forward into the less obvious, more difficult-to-comprehend situations and signals.

Viewing animal communication in this light removes the signaling system from intent on the part of the animal. During the mating season animals do not change color patterns with the intention of announcing sexual readiness. The signal simply appears at the appropriate time. Other animals recognize it for what it is, and whether they do so innately or through learning is immaterial to this discussion. The same rules apply to the sound and chemical-emission systems of animals.

Before analyzing communication processes in any context, knowledge of both emitting and receiving parts of the system must be acquired. In studying any animal, human or other, the scientist or student should pass through a fairly circumscribed set of procedures, the first part of which is a close examination of what is termed "normative behavior."

This means long-term and detailed observation of all sexes and ages, which provides some understanding of the world in which that particular species lives. Is the species under study social, nonsocial, or seasonally variable? At what age is it adult? How much parental care do the adults of either sex administer? What does it eat? What are the limits of its spatial or other territorial requirements before aggression appears? Questions of this kind must be answered both in the field and in the laboratory to avoid foolish, wasteful, and frequently erroneous experimental procedures. Fortunately for the researcher, these basic questions have been answered for many species of wildlife and he need not spend more than a limited time reading the literature and comparing his own observations with what he has read. He then knows the unanswered and unresolved questions and can proceed fairly quickly into his own experimental work.

So little of such basic information on dolphins has been obtained that these studies have to continue even while other problems are being investigated. The reasons for this will become particularly obvious to the reader as the following discussion of the dolphins' sensory and communication system proceeds.

Until we understand an animal's sensory and perceptual system fairly well, we have little hope of entering its world. For example, several people have shown that dolphins in general are sensitive to and respond to tones of 150,000 cycles per second. A human with good hearing perceives up to only 20,000 cycles per second. If dolphins ran tests on humans using 50,000 cycles per second tones as intelligence testing devices, we would be tossed aside by their scientists as a species totally unable to learn or even be conditioned. They might be right in their conclusions, judging by our behavior at times, but they would be incorrect to test us by that method, because we would be completely unaware that they were even playing sounds. A dog scientist would no doubt think first of testing us by using odors, and we would fail his tests miserably.

Both from experimental evidence and from what logic would lead us

99

to expect, we are on pretty firm ground in stating that the dolphin's world is primarily a world of sound. The strong development of the appropriate lobes of the dolphin brain further suggests this. But even as we live primarily in a world of vision and continue to make use of sound, smell, touch, and taste, so dolphins continue to use at least some of these and other sensory systems.

Hearing. To date science has experimentally tested to any degree only one of the dolphin's senses—that of hearing. As already stated, we know that they can hear sound of up to 150,000 cycles per second. There is still considerable controversy as to *how* dolphins hear. While they have an obvious external ear opening, it is so tiny that many researchers do not believe that this is the primary pathway for the reception of sound.

Surprising as the idea at first may seem, a large percentage of the workers in this field now subscribe to the theory that sound is received through the lower jaw. There are large nerve endings in this region that seem to have no other obvious function, especially since they lead back to other tissues which in turn lead to the complex and fully developed internal ear. The lower jaw is filled with a near-liquid fat, and this substance may help direct the sound from the receptor areas in the jaw to the inner ear. Experimental work has given considerable credence to this theory.

Our own recent experiences tend to make us give this hypothesis more consideration than we did previously. One of our experimental dolphins (a juvenile male) was being trained to find the source of sound being played underwater into his tank through a special underwater transmitter called a transducer. So that he could not see the transducer, the dolphin was also trained to wear blindfolds (harmless soft rubber suction cups placed comfortably over his eyes). When he approached the transducer as it emitted sounds, instead of touching it with the tip of his snout as he usually did to indicate a positive choice in other kinds of (nontransducer) experiments, he laid his lower jaw against the instrument

To test echolocation, dolphins are trained to wear blinders. (Marineland of the Pacific)

as if to receive the vibrations the speaker was sending out. The dolphin had to turn on his side and back to do this, and he kept his lower jaw pressed against the transducer's speaker much longer than would be expected if he were merely touching it to confirm its presence or the fact that it was the source of the sound. The dolphin gave every indication of listening to the transducer with his lower jaw.

Sound Production. Although apparently not true of all species of dolphins and porpoises, bottlenosed dolphins produce two basic kinds of sounds, those that consist of a series of distinct pulses and those that resemble a pure tone. The pulsed sounds in turn are broken down into those regular series of clicks which are used for environmental exploration or echolocation, and those bursts of clicks which we often term "burst pulse sounds" and which we believe are communicative since they vary with the kind of behavior the dolphin is manifesting when they are emitted. The "pure tone" sound, or whistle, apparently is used for certain kinds of communication and it is this class of sound that only certain species of dolphins are known to produce.

Today, the most generally accepted theory of dolphin sound production holds that all phonations are generated within the nasal sac system

101

(a series of air-filled pouches) lying just beneath the surface of the skin around the blowhole. Dolphins are known to generate both pulsed sounds and whistles simultaneously, indicating two separate mechanisms within the nasal sac system for the generation of these two types of sound. Most scientists working in the field of sound production believe the role of the larynx is zero, or at best grossly reduced. There are several reasons for this view, not the least of which is the complete absence of vocal cords in this nonconformist mammalian group. Since all dolphins (and other kinds of cetaceans) have evolved so many highly specialized adaptations to their underwater environment, the scientists who study them have had to be able to rid themselves of their preconceived notions gathered from land-dwelling animals. The study of sound production and reception is a particularly difficult hurdle to surmount.

The upper surface of the dolphin skull forms a concave dish below the nasal sac system, and this concavity varies tremendously among different kinds of dolphins; some are very shallow, while others almost form a tunnel. There is a general relationship between a dolphin species' ecological or anatomical needs for echolocation and the degree of concavity of the dish. Species living in clear, open ocean waters usually have skulls in which this concavity is shallow. Species that spend much of their

A whistling dolphin frequently, but not always, emits air from its blowhole. (Marineland of Florida)

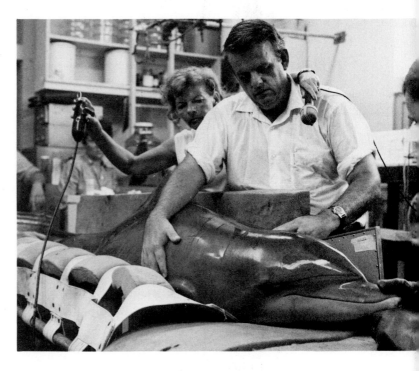

The authors make sound recordings while a phonating dolphin is X-rayed in trying to learn something of the mechanisms whereby such sounds are produced. (Marineland of Florida)

time in murky waters, as does the bottlenosed dolphin, have a skull with a moderately deep concavity. In species that are totally blind, as is the freshwater dolphin of the Ganges and other Indian rivers, the skull bone almost forms a tunnel. The concavity of the skull is believed to function as an aid in directing *outgoing* echolocation clicks, and consequently the beam is narrower in those species needing to have more control over their use of echolocation in environmental exploration. The deeper the concavity of the skull, the more directed the beam of clicks can be.

Dolphins are vocal in air as well as underwater. They whistle and squawk at humans with the same degree of enthusiasm (or lack of enthusiasm when protesting) as they do toward each other. Their "protest squawk," emitted as a complaint sound, is the vocalization that trainers reinforce and sometimes shape toward some faint degree of similarity to our human words. Usually, however, the training method involved consists of quickly tossing a fish reward to the dolphin for making the squawk, then building a trick around the animal's normal sounds. The dolphin "singing" acts are an example of such training techniques.

103

Echolocation and Sound Localization. Probably no part of the experimental study of dolphins has received so much attention in recent years as their ability to echolocate. The principles involved are much the same as those used by the Navy in sonar, or the land and air forces in radar. Simply, it is a matter of sending out a sound signal and recording the direction from which an echo is received back at the sending station and the time it took to receive it to determine the location of the object being scanned. Essentially this is echolocation, but in addition to location, the returning echo may yield much more information, like the size, shape, and consistency of the target.

The suggestion that dolphins might be echolocating was first made some years ago when it was discovered that they were able to avoid capture nets even though the water was so murky that they could not possibly have seen the nets. Furthermore, the dolphins were turning away *before* they touched them. The size of the meshes in the net proved to be important—the larger the spaces and the finer the twine used to make them, the harder it was for the dolphins to avoid them.

A few years after this, experiments conducted separately by William E. Schevill and Dr. Barbara Lawrence (Mrs. Schevill) and by Dr. Winthrop N. Kellogg demonstrated that dolphins were able to find objects in the water by echolocation. Not only were the dolphins able to find an object, but they could discriminate between sizes or material, even to selecting a preferred kind of fish over another of the same size. More recently, Dr. Kenneth S. Norris and his associates have made many contributions to the field of dolphin echolocation by using various experimental approaches. Much that we know about the details of the dolphin sonar system is derived from his results and those of the various teams he has coordinated to investigate specific questions. Many of the procedures are too technical to fall within the scope of this book, but details can be found in the writings of Dr. Norris (who cites the earlier studies) listed in "Suggested Reading Lists" on page 152. A few salient facts indicating the beauty and complexity of the system are in order here, however.

A blindfolded dolphin can clear a barrier by using its ability to echolocate needed landmarks. (Marineland of the Pacific)

Sonar or echolocation clicks are usually beamed directionally toward the object the dolphin is investigating. The frequency of cycles-per-second, duration, and rapidity of the clicks can be varied widely, according to the animal's needs of the moment. The clicks are capable of being emitted and the echo received and processed within the dolphin's brain with such rapidity that the actual figures become as meaningless to our comprehension, as do the enormous figures involved in distances to other star systems. Several hundred clicks a second may be produced, some clicks being as brief as 0.0001 second. There is good evidence that the echo from each click is processed prior to the next click emission. All of this adds up to a pretty fair computer in anyone's book.

Tone pips can be resolved by the animal's brain if separated by a 0.001-second time interval. That means a capability of processing at a single site 1,000 bits of this information in one second. Other types of sound information are of course being processed simultaneously at other sites in the brain—no one as yet knows where or how.

105

A dolphin's echolocation is so precise that a blindfolded animal was once able to find half of a vitamin pill on the bottom of its tank. Echolocation is not only a marvelous adaptation, it also indicates the tremendous ability of the dolphin's brain to make the necessary fine discriminations. A computer the size of a room probably could not do as good a job even if we knew what information to give it. The Navy has become very interested in research on this subject as it might be applied to their own sonar systems. Researchers working on problems of the human blind have studied the findings in the hope that they may aid in developing an electronic sonar or radar system that a blind person could carry with him to help him through his dark world. Consequently, the emphasis of research on dolphin echolocation is on learning the means by which they do it and the significant structure of their echolocation sound pulses.

Dolphins not only have this excellent ability to pinpoint objects by means of active echolocation, but they are also able to locate passively the origin of sound sources underwater with uncanny ability. It is likely that the same or similar brain areas which process returning echos of their own sending during the process of echolocation also process sound emissions generated by some other underwater source.

Since human ability to localize the source of sound underwater is very poor, it is the dolphin's ability to locate direct sound sources underwater that offers potential for their use, in addition to their possible assistance in finding lost humans or inanimate objects at sea.

Vision. Although dolphins are able to explore their environment by means of echolocation, they give every indication of being fully able to see well both in and out of water. There once was some question about their out-of-water vision, as indicated in earlier literature, but anyone working with dolphins soon becomes aware that they can see very well. They are able to catch a small ball thrown from a distance of 25 feet or so, and are able to jump vertically as high as 16 feet or more

Even while making an unusual leap, a dolphin has the ability to pluck a fish unerringly from its trusting trainer's mouth. (Florida Gulfarium)

and snatch a suspended object. They perform both feats with unerring accuracy.

We have had a few brief and somewhat weak indications that some degree of echolocation in air may be involved at times, but the fact that a dolphin coming close to an object turns its head so that one eye focuses on it (turning the head would direct the forward-projecting echolocation beam away from the object) indicates to us that vision is the primary sense involved in such circumstances.

When investigating objects that are farther than a few feet away, a dolphin usually faces the object head on, which would put it in a position either to use stereoscopic vision or to direct its echolocation beam at it.

107

The eyes of a dolphin apparently can be directed forward to give it stereoscopic vision. (Marineland of Florida)

Animals looking out from behind a glass, on the other hand, as they often do, would find their echolocation system useless, because the glass would deflect it. Inasmuch as the dolphin, by its behavior, is obviously perceiving the subject beyond the glass sufficiently well to hold its attention, it must be doing so visually.

In an informal study, more out of playful curiosity on our part than anything else, we recently placed a television set so that our juvenile male dolphin could see it through a window in the side of his tank or by placing his head over the rim of the tank. We then stood back so as not to distract him and made observations on his attention to the programs, which we could monitor. The experiments were conducted at night to further reduce his distractions and also to obtain a better picture on the screen. From his attention, there was no doubt that he was watching the picture. There also was no question that he paid more attention to some programs than to others—he preferred variety programs and commercials to dramatic sequences. One incident in particular bore this out one evening when our assistants Nick and Hazel Hall were conducting the tests.

Just after a program change, and at a moment when their own attention was distracted away from the monitor, the dolphin suddenly began swimming rapidly around in the tank, vocalizing loudly, and violently tossing his ball high into the air again and again. This ball, it might be mentioned, had been his favorite toy for many months, and he always took every opportunity to play with it by himself or especially to induce humans to play catch or swim and retrieve with him with it. Wondering what all the commotion was about, and fearing that something terrible must be wrong, Nick and Hazel rushed to the side of the tank. Instead of a catastrophe, they found that a baseball game was being televised, and a ball was being thrown back and forth between several players in such a manner that it was clearly visible on the screen.

Although the conclusion must be subjective, of course, there was every reason to believe that the dolphin was excited by the ballgame that he could see on the screen and so began to play with his own ball. Inasmuch as the men on the screen would neither throw him their ball, or return his when he offered it, he became progressively more excited and began to vocalize and swim rapidly around in his tank. This is exactly the behavior that he exhibits toward us if we frustrate him by not playing ball with him when he offers. While the results are only preliminary, we feel that this project deserves more attention (using closed-circuit television wherein we or the dolphin can control the subject on the screen for objective studies) and that it will lead to a greater understanding of the visual (and other) capabilities of this dolphin species.

Although attempts have been made to study the ability of dolphins to see color, we know of no well-documented results to show whether they can or cannot. It is obvious to people working with them that they often react more to one hue than to another, but this seems to be an individual thing in which one animal might be fearful of white, while another seems afraid of black. While the results of experiments in color discrimination have been disappointing (so far primarily the results of difficulties in experimental technique), other experiments in the ability of dolphins to visually discriminate patterns have been more successful.

They are able to do this, and further evidence shows that they are indeed able to see and discriminate finite forms and patterns, and not merely attend to motion as some observers have suggested.

Touch. The dolphin's sense of touch is also obviously well developed, as anyone who watches dolphins for very long will see. They engage in considerable body contact with one another—touching flippers, rubbing their bodies against one another, caressing one another with their flippers and flukes, and gently nipping and mouthing one another. They also rub themselves on the bottom of their tanks or on brushes, anchored, bristles up.

Smell and Taste. All of the anatomical evidence points to the conclusion that dolphins lack the sense of smell. There are no olfactory lobes in the brain. However, observational data suggest that they may have a sense of taste. Inasmuch as taste and smell are so closely allied in other mammals (we humans, for instance, cannot taste very well when our sense of smell is completely blocked), it can be asked if dolphins don't have some physiological means (chemoreceptors) for detecting air- and water-borne chemicals that at least give them the capabilities characteristic of taste and smell as we think of these senses in land mammals.

We have a clue there may be chemoreceptors in the dolphin's blowhole—the anatomical equivalent of nostrils—or associated respiratory tract. The blowhole is on top of the head, simplifying air breathing for the animal as it comes to the surface, and is opened but rarely under water. We once were carrying some newly captured dolphins on a truck. During the first hour, over a route of 50 miles or so, they had vocalized only a little, but when we ran through a cloud of mosquito spray they began to vocalize in almost a frenzy. Although the spray may have been physically irritating to their lungs, we humans did not find it particularly so. The odor was pungent, however, and this, combined with the fact that it was probably a new experience for the dolphins, suggests that

As a juvenile male bottlenosed dolphin and an adult eastern Pacific whitesided dolphin rub together in play, both emit whistles, as shown by the two streams of air bubbles. (David K. Caldwell)

An eastern Pacific pilot whale scratches itself on an anchored brush just as bottlenosed dolphins do. (Marineland of Florida)

some sense related to smell, if not pain, was involved. Regardless of how, there is no doubt that the dolphins detected some foreign chemical in the air.

We stated earlier that the genital region of a newly introduced dolphin is examined closely by the residents of the community. We and others have found pores in the male genital area (albeit rarely) whose function, if any, has not been satisfactorily explained. It is possible that they exude some sort of material (like musk in some land mammals), which in turn may serve some chemical function in identification by taste by the investigating dolphin, and thus give a behavioral result similar to the smelling of musk by land mammals.

Communication. The considerable attention that has been given to communication in dolphins in the past decade unfortunately has not emphasized the biological aspects of communication by dolphins among themselves. Instead, the emphasis has been on the premise that dolphins can talk and that they do this readily with any human who is willing to listen. Dolphins do of course communicate with other dolphins, and especially precocious ones even establish communication of sorts with their human attendants, but dolphins do not talk.

Even though they don't talk, dolphins may prove more valuable to us in communication studies than a talking animal would be. All of us who work in cetology can be thankful for public interest in dolphins because this misinformation may make it easier for us to obtain funds for research. It has also forced us to dig really deep to find out what all their phonations are about in order to be able to prove to even the most fanatical believers that dolphins do not talk. In doing so we may have had to burst a few balloons (including some of our own), but we have uncovered some facts which make it all worth while to us and which we hope in the long run will be beneficial to mankind. While the work is not yet advanced enough to make unequivocal statements, we can say that there is good reason to believe that we can tell much of the dolphin's emotional state (as contrasted to his physiological state of hunger or pain, for example) by listening to the quality of its vocalizations. If this is true, it will give us an experimental model whereby we hope to be able to measure emotional states in humans merely by listening to a burst of speech. The clinical and other practical uses for this ability are immense. A psychologist would likely be able to detect the true emotional state of a patient who tried to disguise it in conversation. A ground control officer could probably tell when a pilot was under pressure that he would not orally admit.

Dolphins do communicate (in the broad sense) certain states of mind and certain needs to an experienced trainer or handler, but the level of communication is on the order of that between a man and his dog. Obviously, some communication is directed toward the human attendant, while in other interactions the attendant is merely able to interpret normal undirected behavior of the dolphin.

An example of direct communication might be when a dolphin brings a toy over to its attendant for a game. The dolphin brings the ball to the man, not to any random spot along the side of the tank. In our experience if the man refuses to move even a foot toward the side to retrieve the ball placed in his vicinity, the dolphin will move the ball to a point directly in front of the man. That the animal will do this again and again, usually until the attendant is exhausted, is evidence of directed behavior—successfully communicating the desire to play.

This playful dolphin shows just how wide the mouth can be opened. (Marineland of Florida)

One wild dolphin tail slaps while its companion observes an intruding boat. Note the masses of barnacles on the tail and dorsal fin of the animal at left, typical of many dolphins seen in the open sea off Florida. (Marineland of Florida)

Similarly, it is often obvious that the dolphin wants the play to proceed a certain way. If the man fails to throw the ball in the preferred fashion, the dolphin may express displeasure by tail slapping the surface of the water, vocalizing in an unusually loud manner, or even hitting at its attendant with its snout. Our own dolphin's patterns of play tend to shift from time to time and it is sometimes difficult for us to understand what game he is trying to teach. When we finally catch on, he seems satisfied to play it *ad nauseam* for days or even weeks until he devises a new variation that we must learn.

One of our experimental animals was sick for a few days and therefore not eager to eat. He expressed this not only by playing with his food and eating very slowly, but also by pushing it away with his snout or even by shoving the feeding bucket away from where it was perched on the side of his tank. One day he even began to return the fish directly to his handler. Thus, although he continued to be playful, the dolphin communicated his illness to us by his simple but obvious actions.

A trainer, on the other hand, might make his displeasure clear to a dolphin pupil by turning his back and walking away when the animal does not perform at a level it is capable of. No physical punishment is used, and no food is withheld, but the dolphin is aware that it has displeased its trainer. The dolphin then often makes very obvious attempts to compensate by doing better the next time or by offering to "make up" to its trainer by coming over to the side of the tank to seek his attention.

The tail slap—mentioned earlier—is an example of natural dolphin behavior that communicates something to humans. Observational studies of dolphin communities, corroborated by observations in the wild, suggest that an angry or disturbed dolphin will lift its tail flukes out of the water and slap them down hard on the surface, making a loud report and transmitting alarm to the herd. The slap appears to be made when the fear is due to some unfamiliar intrusion into the dolphin's territory. In captivity, the introduction of a new training prop may elicit a tail slap. A frustrating situation such as lack of an expected reward may result in a tail slap directed so that the flying water will drench the trainer. The man has no doubt in his mind that the dolphin is communicating with him on that basis, and it is a correct interpretation on his part.

Dolphins communicate with one another by making sounds and in other perhaps less obvious behavioral ways.

We have already discussed the production of sound and the three basic types of sounds that dolphins produce as "phonations"—we now really prefer not to call them "vocalizations" since the method of production is somewhat different from that of most mammals. A few of the sounds that bottlenosed dolphins emit are specific to certain emotional states. For example, one such sound in particular—a sharp crack produced as a very broad-band, pulsed sound—appears to be elicited as a startled response to an immediate and sudden danger. Another has been termed a sex yelp and apparently accompanies a male's premating behavior.

Even the regular trains of clicks used in echolocation must contribute to carrying information, as a dolphin echolocating rapidly on a fish signals this fact to other members of its herd. Merely by emitting this sound, it has alerted the others to a possible source of food. By and large, non-echolocation pulsed sounds (burst-pulse sounds) appear to be associated with a particular type of behavior and seem almost to be the result of it, somewhat like laughter among children at play or a grunt emitted when a boxer is hit by his opponent. Each individual bottlenosed dolphin apparently makes approximately the same kind of burst-pulse sounds under given behavioral situations that another bottlenosed dolphin would under the same conditions—the sounds, then, appear to be more common to the species than to the individual.

There is great need for further research, however, for most of the sounds produced and the behaviors observed do not correlate 100 per cent. Instead, there is an over-all tendency for sounds to grade from one to another as the emotional level of the animal changes, much in the same manner as chasing may blend from play into a fight.

We find that almost all dolphins have an individual recognizable signature whistle that is unique and by which it can almost always be recognized. We have tested a male dolphin to make certain that he could recognize the individual whistles of other dolphins as well as we can recognize them. In this type of experiment the animal presses a paddle with his snout on certain whistles but not on others. We made tape recordings of the whistles of individual animals under a wide variety

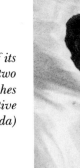

During an experimental study of its ability to discriminate between two different sounds, a dolphin pushes a paddle to indicate a positive choice. (Marineland of Florida)

of conditions and then dubbed these onto another tape, mixing the whistles of several other dolphins among those he was to select. The dolphin almost unerringly selected the whistles of specific animals from a complex array of other animals' whistles.

The dolphin used in these experiments could 100 per cent of the time single out one individual's whistle from a continuously running tape containing the whistles of eight other animals. He could also pick out all of the whistles of four different animals from a tape which contained a great assortment of many different whistles from a total of eight animals. This particular set of experiments was then discontinued since the dolphin seemed to have made his point—he was capable of recognizing a great many dolphins on the basis of their "whistle-voices" alone. When we tested the animal again 8 months later on these same whistles, he remembered them perfectly.

In another set of experiments he demonstrated that he could distinguish between the whistles of other animals 100 per cent of the time if he could hear them for only one-half second. So we no longer had to worry about the fact that perhaps we could tell dolphin whistles apart better than a dolphin could.

Rarely we do find a dolphin whose whistles are variable even to our own ears and to our sound-analyzing equipment. Our dolphin could pick out the whistles of one of these animals only 80 per cent of the time.

Dolphin whistles are largely so constant to the individual that we had been fairly well convinced for many years that they could not voluntarily change the basic structure of their own particular "whistle-voice." Our experimental dolphin killed this theory very recently when he began to mimic very precisely a 10,000-cycle-a-second pure tone sound that we had been playing to him underwater. We frankly don't know what to do about this little piece of hypothesis-shattering data except to report that it occurred. We should specify very clearly, however, that this is the only time that we personally have encountered it.

At times of particular stress the dolphin may produce what we term a

117

"whistle-squawk," wherein a loud pulsed sound is made concurrently with the whistle. We have found such phonations to be emitted in protest, as when a dolphin has been removed from the water for treatment or examination. This sound, too, is often specific to an individual, and not only is the signature whistle of the animal emitted, but the squawk (a burst-pulse sound) begins and ends at the same points in time in relation to the form of the whistle.

Whistles certainly convey something of the emotional state of the whistler. Loneliness or the desire to be reunited with a parent or offspring might be communicated through a long series of very loud whistles produced very rapidly. The dolphin may increase the pitch and loudness when in panic. The duration of the whistle might vary under different emotional circumstances, from a very short fragment called a "chirp" to a very long sequence repeated without break. Within these boundaries, then, and with the exceptions just noted, we have found that the signature-whistle hypothesis holds. The communicative value is based on variations in the rapidity of emission and manner of production of this signature whistle. Contrary to the suggestion of some writers, we do not believe that a particular dolphin behavior has a specific species-wide kind of whistle associated with it—as a "distress call"—but instead that the distress is conveyed in the manner in which that individual's signature whistle is emitted. The whistle is unique to the individual dolphin, the way in which it is used conveys the desired information.

Prior to the panic stage, the whistle does tend to become more brief, less intense, and less frequently emitted as fear increases. Just as the jungle goes silent when a predator appears, so does the dolphin tank when danger threatens. This very silence then is a form of communication, for it represents a holding back (inhibition) of normal whistling in the presence of danger, and the other dolphins recognize it for what it is. When the danger passes or becomes so intense that there is no more value in staying silent, the inhibition in the animals is either lost

118

or overcome and an abnormal amount of whistling may occur immediately.

Dolphins sometimes produce sounds other than those termed "phonations." These, too, are communicatory. Probably the most common is the jaw clap, made when the animal forcefully snaps its jaws together and produces a sharp cracking sound. Usually made as a threat to another dolphin, it also has been directed toward human divers when a dolphin has been cornered or chased. Dolphins may release a large bubble of air from the blowhole underwater, which makes a noticeable gurgling sound as it rises to the surface. The context here is unclear, but seems to be related to excitement such as that induced by imminent feeding or special curiosity aroused when a diver engages in some unusual underwater activity.

The act of swimming rapidly also produces a relative increase in sound, and other dolphins in the area might well take a clue from this that some danger is present. Under disturbed conditions, dolphins sometimes exhale air on the surface in a typical noisy burst or snort. These snorts also are heard clearly underwater. Finally, dolphins may swim rapidly with most of the head out of water as if to see objects or activities farther away or otherwise out of range of their underwater sensory capabilities. This behavior is indicative of an aroused emotional state in the animal, and often is accompanied by considerable splashing induced by its awkward position. Such splashing would indicate some unusual activity to other dolphins nearby.

Dolphins may communicate by touch or sight as well as by sounds. A cow giving her calf a hard nip certainly communicates her displeasure with it, whereas a gentle nipping is affectionate or playful. Body position is an important means by which one dolphin signals to another, and we have seen a dominant cow merely turn and face other individuals to stop them from pursuing some behavior that she apparently disliked.

In our own experience, and in that of other workers, we have known individual dolphins to spend either brief or long periods lying on the

A juvenile dolphin emits a burst of bubbles as it receives a sharp bite from a shark-scarred cow. (David K. Caldwell)

bottom of their tanks balanced on their flippers and flukes. Sometimes this has been related either to a disturbance in the tank (a young animal did this, as if sulking after receiving an injection) or to typical behavior of an individual. For example, a young male at Florida's Gulfarium became known as Rip Van Winkle because he spent so much time on the bottom and appeared to be asleep, rising only to breathe. Such behavior undoubtedly is noticed by other members of the dolphin community and possibly conveys some information not yet clear to us.

Visual communication in dolphins is expressed not only actively but also passively through certain markings. The tip of the snout in bottle-nosed dolphins, especially older ones, is usually white, or at least a lighter gray than the rest of the snout, and then there is often the white or lighter gray area around the genital region. It is believed that these lighter areas serve as recognition marks, and if this is so, the marking is probably more on a species than an individual basis. Different species

120

The lighter genital region clearly shows on this jumping female. (David K. Caldwell)

of dolphins have different kinds of markings that stand out in cloudy or murky water. Such marks would alert the observing individual not only to the presence of another individual but also its species in situations where different species mix.

Although further study may show that there is more to these white markings than simple recognition, there is at present no good evidence for a sexual difference, as might be expected. The marks do become more obvious as the animals grow older, however, and a recognizable age difference may thus be communicated to the other members of the herd. Such information might help individuals recognize specific individuals in the group, or members of established hierarchies which to a large degree appear to be related in their structure to the size (and, consequently, age) of the animals involved. Inasmuch as newly introduced animals go immediately to the genital region of one another, it seems possible that the illumination (through light reflected off the lighter markings) of this part of the body in the often murky waters of

121

the wild habitat might be an advantage to dolphins in this early recognition stage. This means of recognition may be coupled with some sort of chemoreception, as noted earlier.

It has been suggested that the lighter genital (and, consequently, mammary) area is necessary to help the infant find its mother's nipples, but because the calf always follows its mother very closely during the early nursing period when such a guide might conceivably be required, we do not feel as strongly about such a need for lighter coloration but do not completely discount the idea. A further basis for our hesitation lies in the fact that very large adult males are also usually light-colored in the genital area, and it is for this reason that we lean toward our age-recognition theory instead.

Shades of gray mark the head of this adult male. (David K. Caldwell)

Color and Color Patterns

DOLPHINS SHOW remarkably little variation in color except for the extent of creamy white coloration on their bellies and for variations in intensity of grays in their basic pattern. At times, some of the lighter areas, especially the light grays on the lower sides, also show a yellowish tint but, like the gray shadings, this is very much an individual sort of thing. In addition to those various shades of gray, we have already mentioned the even more prominent light regions on the body around the tip of the snout and the anal region that may be useful as age and/or specific recognition marks. Many of the darker (and lighter) streaks appear to be related to water-flow patterns over the body, but these remain to be studied and analyzed in much greater detail. Finally, we have often observed a thin light line leading from a light-colored semicircle around the posterior (rear) edge of the eye socket to the tiny external opening of the ear, which itself may be very light in color. This light line may then extend backward and downward to the rear base of the flipper, or may stop at the ear with a second light line, that has its origin at the eye socket somewhat forward and below the takeoff point for the first line, extending to the base of the flipper. Like the light coloration of the tip of the snout and the anal region in many individuals, this line from eye to flipper and/or eye to ear opening is often extremely conspicuous and may serve as a recognition mark. The eyes of the normally colored animals are dark brown.

123

A juvenile male shows his Himalayan pigmentation. (Wometco Miami Seaquarium)

Albino bottlenosed dolphins are known, but not any pure black (melanistic) ones. Some are a very dark variation of the normal coloration. Interestingly, the darkest animals that we have seen pictures of were ones that appeared to be the calves of the lighter animals such as the near-albinos or other light-colored variants. This is not because these young stand out darkly against the lighter mother; they have a truly darker pigment. We have also noted that these are calves that are no longer in the newborn stage, during which the young usually are darker than their mothers.

An almost white, but darkly mottled, adult female swims with a dolphin of more normal color. (Marineland of Florida)

The adult female at the bottom is the only dolphin covered with tiny flecks of pigment like this that we have ever seen. (Marineland of Florida)

The variation in degree of darkness is real, and not a trick of the camera or lighting. (David K. Caldwell)

In addition to pure albino bottlenosed dolphins, which have pink eyes, we have seen: (1) buff or cream-colored ones with dark red eyes; (2) almost white ones with black specks and mottled areas and, apparently red, eyes; (3) ones with the so-called Himalayan coloration, which consists of a dark strip down the center of the back, dark flippers, dark points on the dorsal fin and flukes, a dark snout, and red eyes; and (4) normally colored ones with dark brown eyes, except that their bodies are covered with tiny dark flecks of pigment.

Color and Color Patterns

Although the number of unusually colored dolphins is low, there is a tendency, as would be expected, for a given color variation or its modifications to reoccur in a rather restricted geographical area. Such color variation is genetically controlled, and if there is limited movement of a population, the inherited factor would also be limited geographically. Since this seems to be true, it provides further evidence of limited movements of dolphin populations. A certain amount of mixing of populations on their geographical edges (gene flow) eventually would move the genes for an unusual color variation, such as a buff color, throughout a large geographical area comprising a major or whole part of the range of the bottlenosed dolphin. However, the scarcity of such unusual color variants, the long gestation and nursing periods of dolphins, the relatively long period before maturity is reached and another generation begun, and the fact that such color mutants in other kinds of animals (and presumably so in dolphins as well) usually are especially subject to predation solely because their color makes them stand out, would all work together to make extended movement of genes for the unusual coloration a very long-term phenomenon.

A newly captured dolphin nears the boat. (Aquatarium)

The web stretcher supports the weight evenly as a dolphin is lifted aboard the mother ship after capture. (Marineland of Florida)

Capture and Adaptation to Captivity

BECAUSE DOLPHINS LIVE IN shallow and protected habitats, it is not too difficult for a practiced crew to encircle a school with a large net, trap them against the shore or boat, and select the animal or animals desired. Once this is done, the others can be released no worse for the experience. The dolphins selected are then lifted gently into a small boat while still in a section of the net. Next they are hoisted by sling either onto a larger boat for transport or directly onto the dock if the catchers have been working near home base.

It has been our experience that most dolphins quickly become quiet as soon as all chance of escape has gone. Even in the net they may lie still and struggle little if handled carefully and gently.

As long as the animals are kept wet and laid on pads, they can be kept out of water for truck or air transport for several days, although it is usually more a matter of hours. Like humans immobilized in hospital beds, the dolphins are turned periodically to help reduce the possibility of pneumonia. As noted elsewhere, they are unlike most mammals in that they do not have sweat glands or other means of ridding themselves of excess body heat and must be kept wet to avoid being literally burned up from the inside.

Once they are in their new home the dolphins seem to adapt quickly to the enclosed environment and never show any evidence of bumping into the wall of the tank. (This is not necessarily true of the sick indi-

129

viduals of other species that are sometimes rescued from the beach.) Because they eat live fish in the wild, it sometimes takes several days to teach dolphins to take dead ones, which circumstances dictate that oceanariums use; but we have seen newly caught dolphins eat a dead fish within minutes after being placed in the tank. How soon they begin to eat the dead fish varies.

While most dolphins present no feeding problem, an occasional animal may go too long without eating and special attention must be given to make it accept food. In one instance in particular, Marineland obtained a rare buff-colored juvenile male along with several normally-colored juveniles, and all were housed in the same holding tank. The head trainer, Fred Lyons, tried everything he could think of to entice them to eat, and even put some live fish in the tank hoping that this would excite them to the point of eating dead ones. Nothing worked, and he was getting desperate. He then did something he had never tried before. Lowering the water level to the point where the dolphins could just swim, he entered the tank and began to gently harass them by throwing fish at them. As many of our readers probably know from experiences with their pet dogs, the dolphins began to snap back—a behavior un-usual in these animals. The harder they snapped, the more fish Fred hit them with until finally he literally began to slap the dolphins on the back with a fish. The dolphins returned this gesture by snapping at his hand, and just as one snapped, Fred jammed a fish into its mouth. It was too late for the dolphin to do anything but swallow it. He won the battle, with each animal attempting to get his hand or leg and finding a fish in its mouth instead. After just one or two such bites, the dolphins began to take fish on their own and also began to clean up those left on the bottom of the tank from Fred's earlier tosses.

Not only do some dolphins eat within minutes after being placed in a tank, some that have been captive for only a few hours allow themselves to be touched without showing any sign of panic, even if there is space enough to avoid the human at the side of the tank. It is a rare individual

Learning to ring a bell. (Marineland of Florida)

that is not fully adapted to captivity within a week or two, provided it has had proper care and daily association with its new human companions. Some become so well adapted that they seem to prefer human company to that of other dolphins. They show every evidence of a happy association with man and, once fully adapted, often will not leave even when given the opportunity. At least this has been the experience of a number of us who have worked closely with dolphins.

An experienced trainer can soon recognize a dolphin that will make a good performer. It is usually one that shows a willingness to be handled and some evidence of natural spirit or aggressiveness. Such an animal adapts quickly to training procedures, and the trainer can develop the routines that are familiar to many readers.

Twothirtytwo accepting a fish reward for a task well done. (Marineland of Florida)

It may take a year or more to train a dolphin, but when the program is completed, the dolphin seems to retain its repertoire. We know of one dolphin that did one of its acts immediately upon request after nearly a 10 year interval. In the meantime it had been doing an entirely different act, although it had been kept in a holding pen where it could see other dolphins do its original series of tricks.

While food rewards are usual in the daily shows to reinforce good behavior, dolphins have been known to perform for only a gesture of kindness, in the form of a pat from their trainers. We even know of one animal that performed an entire complicated routine without any reward whatsoever, and it was all that the handlers could do to keep ahead of it with the props for the next act.

It should also be noted here that by the end of the day the dolphins usually have eaten their daily quota of food in the form of rewards for good behavior. However, if an animal does not perform satisfactorily and is not rewarded immediately, the dolphin is still fed its full daily ration at the end of the day. Not to do so is poor husbandry, and furthermore the animal has learned already by the withholding of immediate reward that its behavior was not up to par.

132

Capture and Adaptation to Captivity

Dolphins appear to prefer to satisfy their trainers, and only rarely do they "go on strike" and await the "free feed off" at day's end. Continued poor behavior in training and performance only results in the withdrawal of the animal from the show, which appears to be punishment in itself; it is not punished by starvation.

It has been demonstrated that dolphins learn from one another. A new animal learns its routine much faster if placed with one that is already experienced. This became obvious at Marineland of the Pacific when a rare species of large dolphin (a false killer whale) was placed in a display tank with trained animals. The false killer whale was soon doing the entire show even though it had received no training and no intentional rewards in the form of food.

We are told that sometimes individual dolphins work well for one trainer only. Such an animal was developed at Marineland of Florida, and then shipped to Sea-Arama Marineworld at Galveston, Texas. Although it appeared in good health and ate well, the dolphin refused to perform. While visiting Sea-Arama on other business Fred Lyons,

Swifty, the female false killer whale that learned a full set of dolphin tricks on her own. (Marineland of the Pacific)

its original trainer, was told of this and he immediately went to look over the animal. Finding nothing apparently wrong with it, he decided to put the dolphin through its paces. The animal performed perfectly for Fred, even though it had been many weeks since the two had worked together. Inasmuch as the dolphin was obviously still useful, it was returned to Florida, where it continued to perform under Fred's direction.

Similar, though not as marked, cases are commonplace at oceanariums. Often when a trainer returns from a vacation, or even a weekend, he finds that his special charges are not doing as well as when he left. Apparently this is because the dolphins have worked with other trainers with whom they do not seem to be in as close harmony, even though the same signals and techniques have been used during the original trainer's absence. We are told that even when an animal works well for several trainers, it appears to work best for the original one. Variation in behavior is due partly to slight variations in teaching methods, but there is good reason to believe that dolphins form attachments to certain trainers that are reflected in their performance.

Even though most trained dolphins take their cues and signals with little if any argument, there are occasions when some very unusual factor within their environment will cause them to fail to perform as well as their trainer desires. Such "rebellious" behavior usually is the result of a natural curiosity that distracts or deters the animal. We can offer two examples from our own experience, and one that also happened at Marineland of Florida, that might well have resulted in "curiosity killing the whale" had not the attendants acted quickly.

One of the dolphins at Marineland gave birth to a calf in her holding tank at one end of the stadium pool. During the next show, which started soon afterward, all the performing dolphins, housed at the far end of the long pool, diverted their attention to the new arrival, and it took considerable patience and effort on the part of the trainers to get the show on the road. Even after the initial inspection of the calf through

Dolphins often permit their trainers considerable liberty. (Aquatarium)

the gate to its holding pen, the animals (including a large pilot whale as well as the other dolphins) frequently interrupted their act to go take another look. This continued throughout the first day, and it was several days before all curiosity subsided and things returned to normal. The audience enjoyed the trainers' exasperation even more than the usual well-run show.

A juvenile male dolphin lived in an isolated tank that had both a window in the side and an abnormally high permanent water level that permitted him to put his head easily out over the side, resting his chin on the rim. Between these two opportunities for "sidewalk superintending" this particular dolphin spent much of his day observing the terrestrial world around him and little that went on escaped his attention. Then, one day after feeding, he did not want to play ball — a post-feeding routine he always insisted on. We soon discovered the reason: his attention was concentrated on a large dragline excavating an area some 50 yards away.

We are told that on one occasion at Marineland a large female pilot whale (really a species of dolphin) became more and more intent on watching the training and show performances involving bottlenosed dolphins in an adjacent tank. There was no guard railing around her own tank at the time, and she would rest her head on the rim of it to watch.

135

As the days went by, her curiosity grew and she lifted and supported more and more of her body out of the water in order to see even better. During one show she slid up and up until she came up too high and leaned too far over the side of the tank. It was too late for her to recover herself, and the attendants could do nothing but join the audience in watching the top-heavy whale as she began to fall, slowly at first, then faster, like a forest giant under the lumberjack's ax. Down she came outside her tank, and it took the combined forces of many extra attendants to pick her up and return her to the water. Although this event happened many years ago, the whale is still performing daily, having suffered no apparent damage except perhaps to her cetacean ego. Her holding tank, however, now has a high and substantial guard rail around it to prevent a repeat of the "day Kay fell out of her tank."

Sometimes dolphins are displeased with the performance of their trainer and show it not only in their direct behavior toward him but also by "redirected" aggression. Dr. Sam Ridgway of the U.S. Navy's Undersea Research and Development Center in California related a story to us about the dolphin Tuffy. It seems that one day while he was delivering objects to a diver stationed underwater, Tuffy did not feel that he had been rewarded by the diver fast enough for a job well done. He immediately swam to the surface and bit his regular trainer. This behavior seemed to be a case of redirected aggression, *away* from the offending diver and toward his more familiar trainer.

Similarly, one of the trained dolphins at Marineland of Florida was not rewarded fast enough to suit her when she performed her show act. Since the trainer was out of reach outside the tank, she bit and slashed at her smaller male tank mate when she returned "home." It was several days before he recovered from his wounds, and we are told that during the harassment the male dolphin gave every indication of saying, "What the heck is going on? What did I do to deserve all this?" (Interactions between members of our own species are sometimes all too similar.)

Above: Even in the early days, special attention was given to dolphins at Marineland of Florida. On the right, the late Arthur McBride, an early leader in studies of dolphin biology and husbandry, watches as Mitch Lightsey feeds a dolphin. (Marineland of Florida)

Below: In 1970, nearly a quarter of a century later, Mitch still feeds some of the Marineland dolphins in addition to his many other duties. That is real perseverance and demonstrates the rapport that one can develop with dolphins. (Marineland of Florida)

Care and Husbandry. Prior to the past three and one half decades or so, dolphins were pretty much a curiosity in captivity. The ones that were displayed were often obtained by accident in a fisherman's net or as the result of a shore stranding, and in general were not considered too valuable. If one was not able to make it on its own, it was quickly given up for lost and very little, if any, effort was made to save it through the application of medicines or other treatment. When the animal died, that was that and it was hauled away.

Today, in addition to the personal attachment that they command, dolphins are expensive to obtain, and even more so to keep. As a result there has developed a demand for information on how to keep those already in captivity alive and in good health.

Physiological and medical requirements of dolphins are so specialized that great effort is being expended on research in dolphin care by a rapidly developing group of specialists. The U.S. Navy, through its Naval Undersea Research and Development Center in California, at times seems to have more accomplished veterinarians working on dolphins than they have dolphins cavorting in the tank. Some of the work of this facility has been maligned by bad publicity, such as the story about training dolphins to carry torpedoes to enemy ships and both dolphin and ship being destroyed. Dolphins have not been trained to do anything of the sort. In fact, the Navy has learned much that will aid oceanariums and other facilities to take even better care of dolphins.

To save a sick dolphin today, as much effort may be expended as would be on any human, just as the best of care is given a beloved, prized, and well-trained dog or race horse.

Anesthesia for dolphins needing surgery has finally been developed. This is a major accomplishment because their needs, under anesthesia, are so specialized. A dolphin's oxygen requirements are roughly equivalent to ours, although not as short term; it does not breathe regularly and involuntarily the way we do. Instead, it takes irregular breaths which each time exchange almost all of the air in its lungs. Its breathing

A dolphin has to put up with a lot sometimes. Here, veterinarian Jesse White looks over his patient. (Wometco Miami Seaquarium)

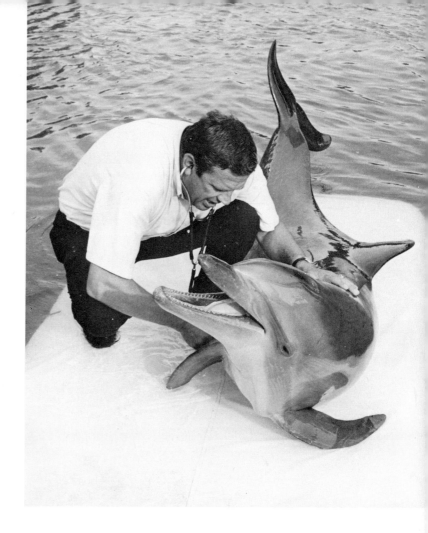

Mass examinations are sometimes required. (Wometco Miami Seaquarium)

can be looked upon as voluntary, and it is this voluntary breathing that helps lead us to believe that dolphins sleep very lightly, if and when they do sleep. Although they can hold their breath for several minutes, which would give them time for a cat nap, a sleeping dolphin would have to awake at least hazily in order to take a fresh breath of air. This unusual method is an adaptation to the underwater environment, but an unconscious or heavily sedated dolphin fails to breathe. Therefore, a very special piece of breathing equipment must be used to supply the animal's now-known needs when it is rendered unconscious.

Dolphin surgery is a new technique, and one that is not yet attempted very often or in very many places. The dolphin's internal organs are so closely packed that the surgeon has to draw a map showing the exact placement of organs for each individual dolphin as he operates, in order to be able to put everything back in exactly the proper place. Dolphins have an unusually streamlined body form, and, unlike most land mammals, have no space for organs to shift around in.

Dolphins are subject to many diseases, and treatment often follows that given to people, especially in the use of antibiotics, vitamins, and the like. Dolphins also suffer accidents, just as we do. One severe problem with dolphins, especially the very young—just as with human babies—is their swallowing of foreign objects. We mentioned this earlier, under the heading of play, but want to emphasize that some individual dolphins are notorious for the habit, and have to be zealously guarded.

At places where dolphins are maintained in tanks, all new employees are warned about the habit, and are subject to dismissal if seen placing an object on the edge of a tank or leaning over one with a small object in hand or pocket. Trainers at Marineland of Florida are forbidden to wear wristwatches since the day a trainer's watch strap broke while he was working with an animal. The watch fell off, only to be swallowed by a valuable dolphin as the timepiece struck the water.

The trainer soon had his watch back, however. While the animal was being caught, some of the Marineland staff went to get a long table to put

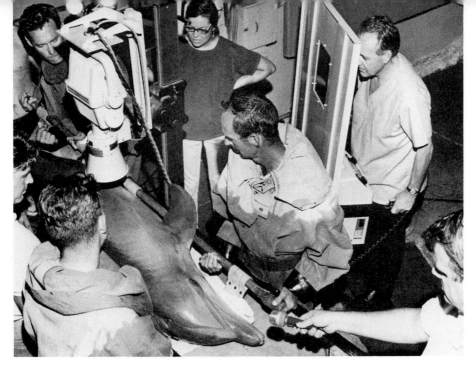

X-ray is used to examine a dolphin for a suspected swallowed object. (Marineland of Florida)

beside the pool. Someone else made a telephone call to Marineland of Florida's chief "swallowed-object-retriever" Cliff Townsend, who is also general manager. Every place that maintains dolphins should have one person with excessively long thin arms that can easily pass down a dolphin's throat. By the time Cliff arrived, the dolphin was on the long table. He reached down the animal's throat, and had the watch at his fingertips within forty-five seconds, but the dolphin had to be tilted before the watch slid into Cliff's hand. The dolphin, no worse off for his experience, continued to be a swallower whenever given the opportunity. No object in the water is overlooked by this dolphin—bugs, leaves, rubber balls, and other objects disappear whenever he is in the pool.

Some dolphins are just the opposite in their behavior and systematically toss every foreign object out of the tank, no matter how insignificant it might seem. No Dutch housewife exceeds the industry with which these tidy tenants remove any small debris from their living quarters. Our own male special research dolphin is a prime example of such behavior. In Florida we are sometimes inundated by half-inch-long insects known locally as flying termites. These insects come out at night and during the early hours of the morning and cover everything. We hap-

141

pened to be working around several dolphin tanks early one morning when such an invasion was in progress. Although the flying insects had ceased to be airborne, the skimming action of the overflow drains of all the dolphin tanks had not yet had time to work and the water surfaces of all but one of these tanks were covered with struggling "termites."

Not so the tank of our dolphin. Not a single termite could be found on the surface of the water in his tank, but the ground around was littered with the waterlogged carcasses of hundreds or even thousands that he had tossed out during the night. He must have been at it full time in order to keep ahead of the invasion, but keep ahead he did—and when the termite horde stopped coming he was the only dolphin left with a clean tank.

The large female false killer whale (at Marineland of the Pacific) that learned the entire trained dolphin show on her own and with no reward, even learned (again on her own) to collect debris in a large community tank and bring it to her tankside attendant for a food reward. Our dolphin that rids his tank of insects often does the same thing just for a pat on the head. If he does not like the food fish we happen to offer him in his regular feeding, he also returns it to the edge of the tank for our disposal, rather than drop it and swim away as do most of his cousins.

Twothirtytwo returns an unwanted mackerel to his trainer. (David K. Caldwell)

Dolphin Strandings

PEOPLE SOMETIMES find themselves faced with the emotionally upsetting problem of what to do when they find a live dolphin stranded on the beach. Very few of us can shrug our shoulders and walk away. Our first instinct is to try to get the dolphin back into the water. Often this is physically impossible because it is too big and heavy and too far from the edge of the water to lift or push it back. Even if someone is successful in getting the animal back into the water, he may be frustrated, perhaps again and again, if the animal refuses to swim away and instead returns almost immediately to strand again. The reasons for this behavior are as yet unknown, but it can recur even after the animal has been towed a mile offshore.

In our experience, strandings of live animals fall into two categories. The first is the stranding of a solitary individual, and we have found for the most part that the animal is sick or injured and that survival is unlikely even with proper handling on the beach and care at an oceanarium. This is not to say that every effort should not be made to rescue it, for not all such animals die. The second category is the mass stranding, and this may mean from two to hundreds of individuals. (A mother and her calf, however, would be considered a single animal because the calf would be expected to follow its mother ashore.) In the mass strandings, the prospect for survival is better for animals that are picked up and taken to an oceanarium, which indicates that all of the animals in such a group are not sick. The number of suggested reasons for such strand-

143

ings almost rivals the number of strandings reported. They range from behavioral reasons, such as panic caused by an attack by sharks, to physiological ones, like failure of the echolocation system.

For the layman, the thing to do if a live stranded animal is found is to have someone call the nearest oceanarium. Almost all will respond to local calls, and some will travel as far as 250 miles or more to try to save an animal. If the oceanarium gives no special instructions to be followed until the arrival of its representatives, the best thing to do is try to get the dolphin into shallow water and hold it upright so that its blowhole will be clear of the water. How deep you can take the animal usually depends on the degree of surf action, but ideally it should almost float in order to relieve the stresses and strains of its own body weight pressing down on its internal organs. If it is too heavy to move, keep the animal wet and cover its exposed eye (if it is on its side) with a wet cloth or paper towel to protect it from the sun and sand. If possible, put it in an upright position, which is more comfortable for it.

The basic thing to remember is that a stranded dolphin should be kept cool, wet, and comfortable. (Keeping it wet usually keeps it cool.) It is not always possible to meet all of these criteria, but you can usually come reasonably close.

If it is being moved in a truck, a good way to keep the animal moist without having a lot of water sloshing around is to cover it with a mixture of hydrous lanolin (better than anhydrous, some believe, because it already has some water in it) and a bit of Vaseline to make the lanolin spread more easily. Every exposed part of the animal should be covered with this mixture but take care not to get it in the eyes and around the immediate lip of the blowhole. Douse it with water if that is all that is available (fresh water is as good as salt water in an emergency). Pay special attention to the tail flukes, dorsal fin, and flippers, and also keep the head moist. You should be careful not to let any water enter the open blowhole during an inspiration. Mr. Nevin Stewart has shipped dolphins from Florida all over the United States and to Europe using only the lanolin-Vaseline mixture, with just enough water in the shipping box to

Methods of transporting dolphins are varied. (Aquatarium)

slosh over the animal's flippers and flukes. The movement of air over the greased body seems to provide the necessary coolness and the water in the lanolin the necessary dampness to keep the skin from overheating from inside and blistering.

Stranded animals that are dead are also useful, and the finder should make every effort to bring such a stranding to the attention of a scientist. Even a badly decomposed animal that is only a mass of ill-smelling tissue and bone often can be utilized by a trained scientist. Much is learned about the distribution of cetaceans from the reporting of strandings, and oftentimes the only specimens of a given species that are seen are stranded ones. If the animal is fresh enough, a great deal can be learned of its biology and food habits by examination of the carcass. Even bleached skulls and other bones on the beach are of value in scientific studies.

In the event a carcass is found near the waterline and there seems to be a danger of its being washed back to sea on the next high tide, haul it high onto the beach if possible, to save it until a biologist can be notified. A dead animal can be buried, but the sands of the beach are constantly shifting and unless the site is very carefully marked, the specimen is likely to be lost. The best thing to do is let someone collect it as it stands rather than try to find it later on after burial. The head is the most valuable single part and every effort should be made to save it, if not the whole animal. Use a knife (an ax will probably do too much damage) and place the head in some safe place until a biologist collects it. If all efforts to keep the specimen itself fail, but photographs can be made, they are of value if good lateral (side) views are made that will permit the identification of the species. Other views are often useful, but in the case of some species it is hard to tell what kind of cetacean is involved without a good over-all lateral view.

With live animals, the nearest oceanarium is the most likely source of help. On the eastern shores of the United States, one might contact (1) the New England Aquarium in Boston, (2) the New York Aquarium on Coney Island, (3) Marineland of Florida near St. Augustine, (4) Ocean World at Ft. Lauderdale, Florida, (5) the Wometco Miami Seaquarium in Miami, (6) the Aquatarium at St. Petersburg Beach, Florida, (7) Florida's Gulfarium at Walton Beach, and (8) Sea-Arama Marineworld at Galveston, Texas. On the Pacific coast, help might be obtained from (1) the Vancouver Public Aquarium in British Columbia, (2) the Steinhart Aquarium in San Francisco, (3) ABC Marine World at Redwood City near San Francisco, (4) Marineland of the Pacific near Los Angeles, and (5) Sea World in San Diego. In Hawaii, Sea Life Park on Oahu is the most active institution.

There are, of course, other local and smaller aquariums that might be interested, but we know that the ones mentioned above have gone for stranded live animals, and often to great distances. Additional marine attractions are either in the construction or planning stages, and since some of these are geographically situated so as to fill gaps in the shore-line not covered by the above, the interested reader may want to keep abreast of these places as possible sources for aid with a live stranded dolphin. All of these institutions are usually aware of biologists interested in obtaining carcasses, and will provide their names and addresses.

Almost any museum or marine laboratory is interested in stranded cetaceans (whales, dolphins, porpoises) both dead and alive. A number of these institutions are equipped to handle and keep live animals, and the others probably can give advice as to what to do or where to go if the stranding is out of the geographical range of one of the organizations noted above. Staff members of museums especially and, to a lesser degree usually, scientists at marine laboratories often go to almost unlimited efforts and distances to recover a dead animal, or a live one too, for that matter, if there is no oceanarium nearby—the effort to save one is always worth the trip. The economics of the situation often make it more likely that the dedicated biologist will go to greater lengths, and usually at his own expense, than the commercial institution's financial considerations allow it to, no matter what the innermost feelings of the local management.

Some of the noncommercial institutions that might be contacted in case of a stranding are (1) the Woods Hole Oceanographic Institution in Massachusetts, (2) the Narragansett Marine Laboratory of the University of Rhode Island at Kingston, (3) the United States National Museum in Washington, D.C., (4) the Duke University Marine Laboratory at Beaufort, North Carolina, (5) the University of Georgia Marine Institute on Sapelo Island near Darien, (6) the School of Marine and Atmospheric Sciences of the University of Miami, (7) the Mote Marine Laboratory at Sarasota, Florida, (8) the Marine Research Laboratory of the Florida Department of Natural Resources at St. Petersburg, (9) the Department of Zoology at Florida State University in Tallahassee, (10) the Gulf Coast Research Laboratory at Ocean Springs, Mississippi, (11) the University of Texas Institute of Marine Science at Port Aransas, (12) the Marine Mammal Biological Laboratory of the U.S. Department of Commerce, Seattle, Washington, (13) the California Academy of Sciences at San Francisco, (14) the Stanford Research Institute at Menlo Park, California, (15) the Natural History Museum of Los Angeles County in Los Angeles, (16) the Cabrillo Museum in San Pedro, California, (17) the San Diego Society of Natural History Museum in San Diego, and (18) the Scripps Institution of Oceanography at La Jolla, California.

These institutions are ones that come to mind as having taken an active interest in cetacean strandings in the recent past. In addition to these, almost any university biology department, state or federal conservation agency or marine laboratory, or local natural history museum or society can recommend an interested biologist if no staff member is interested. Such organizations are distributed widely on or near both coasts of North America, including Canada and Mexico, and they are usually adequately listed in local telphone directories.

Commerce

EXCEPT FOR a few very limited spots in the world, there is little commercial exploitation of any dolphin species except as animals for aquariums and performing shows. Even in places where human populations are high and protein supplies limited, we know of no commercial operations conducted exclusively for the sale of the flesh of bottlenosed dolphins. They are taken, however, in general small-cetacean fisheries operated primarily for food and oil. These are for the most part widely scattered in the more underdeveloped parts of the world.

At the turn of the century and before, a commercial operation exploiting bottlenosed dolphins was conducted in North Carolina in the Cape Hatteras region, primarily for dolphin oil and hides used for leather.

Dolphins were not always treated with care, as this victim of a St. Augustine hunt about 1918 clearly demonstrates. Local fishermen considered them competitors in those days. (Jerry Foreman).

Unfortunately, no serious biological study was made then on the carcasses of the captured animals, and tremendous amounts of good data were lost. Today we rely mostly on beach-stranded animals for studies of this species that require "wild" carcasses.

The lack of dolphin fisheries is primarily due to economic reasons, although the powerful appeal that they have to many people, and the superstitions, myths, and omens of good luck with which seamen associate them are certainly factors. To kill dolphins for any reason is unthinkable to most people. Movements are afoot to curtail even the present use of these animals for public display and research, but there is no evidence that the population, of bottlenosed dolphins at least, is being reduced by these limited captures. We have estimated that in Florida, where most bottlenosed dolphins are captured for use all around the United States and in Europe, less than 1 per cent of a very productive population is harvested.

The few captives that exist provide scientists with an excellent source of knowledge and appreciation for dolphins which we would not acquire otherwise. We learn much from them that shows a potential for application to human problems and their solution. And finally, the entertainment that dolphins offer is not one-sided, for they seem to enjoy our antics as much as, or more than, we enjoy theirs.

Trainer Fred Lyons with Lily, one of his prize pupils. (Marineland of Florida)

Suggested Reading Lists

THE SOURCE for the majority of our remarks in the text of this book has been from our own experience, although some (especially those relating to other scientists' experiments) have been taken from the technical literature. However, we would like to suggest some additional sources containing more details of certain parts of dolphin biology than we have included. In addition to direct studies of dolphins, some of the works listed here have extensive bibliographies of technical papers. The list is thus intended as a source of more general material for lay readers, and for readers wanting to delve more deeply into a given dolphin subject, it is useful as a starting point. Many of the works included should be available in a large public library, and more in a large university library.

A. *For general popular reading on dolphins we suggest:*

Alpers, Antony. *Dolphins: The Myth and the Mammal.* Boston: Houghton Mifflin, 1961. 268 pp. (Still the best general book for adults.)

Chapin, Henry. *The Remarkable Dolphin and What Makes Him So.* New York: Young Scott Books, 1962. 96 pp. (Simple but satisfactory account with some interesting drawings.)

de Narvaez, Cynthia. *My Dear Dolphin.* New York: American Heritage Press, 1969. 64 pp. (Leans too strongly to the adage that "dolphins are people," but contains some interesting photographs.)

Devine, Eleanore and Martha Clark. *The Dolphin Smile.* New York: The Macmillan Co., 1967. 370 pp. (An interesting compilation, not always carefully credited, of dolphin anecdotes and data with only a few, but some good, photographs.)

Jacobs, Lou, Jr. *Wonders of an Oceanarium.* San Carlos, California: Golden Gate Junior Books, 1965. 80 pp. (Not restricted to dolphins, but some especially good dolphin photographs are included.)

Kay, Helen. *The Secrets of the Dolphin.* New York: The Macmillan Co., 1964. 120 pp. (Very good for the young reader.)

Lauber, Patricia. *The Friendly Dolphins.* New York: Random House, 1963. 81 pp. (Excellent children's book with some good photographs.)

Matthews, Leonard Harrison, and others. *The Whale.* New York: Simon and Schuster, 1968. 287 pp. (An elaborate and well-illustrated general work containing considerable valuable data.)

Riedman, Sarah R., and Elton T. Gustafson. *Home Is the Sea: For Whales.* Chicago: Rand McNally, 1966. 264 pp. (A satisfactory general book for adults and advanced juveniles with some good photographs.)

Stenuit, Robert. *The Dolphin, Cousin to Man.* New York: Sterling Publishing Co., 1968. 176 pp. (Text not highly recommended for it contains a number of errors, but book contains some interesting photographs.)

B. *For general or specifically limited subject matter, more technical than the above, yet quite readable, we suggest:*

Andersen, Harald T. (ed.). *The Biology of Marine Mammals.* New York: Academic Press, 1969. 511 pp. (Contains several contributed review papers on various phases of dolphin biology, generally excellent.)

Burt, William H., and Richard P. Grossenheider. *A Field Guide to the Mammals.* Boston: Houghton Mifflin Co., 1952. 200 pp. (Contains a useful section on dolphin identification which includes good drawings of species expected in American waters.)

Busnel, Rene-Guy (ed.). *Animal Sonar Systems, Biology and Bionics.* Jouy-en-Josas, France: Laboratoire de Physiologie Acoustique, 1967. Vol. 1, 713 pp.; Vol. 2, 520 pp. (Contains a number of excellent reviews of research on dolphin echolocation and related pulsed sounds.)

Collins, Henry H., Jr. *Complete Field Guide to American Wildlife.* New York: Harper and Brothers, 1959. 683 pp. (Contains a limited section on the identification of dolphins that might be expected in American waters.)

Daugherty, Anita E. *Marine Mammals of California.* Sacramento, California: State of California Department of Fish and Game, 1965. 87 pp. (Despite the apparently restrictive title the species of dolphins involved are widespread in American waters; a useful booklet.)

Delyamure, S. L. *Helminthofauna of Marine Mammals.* Jerusalem: Israel Program for Scientific Translations, 1968. 522 pp. (A good summary of dolphin parasites is included; published originally in Russian.)

Fraser, F. C. "Whales and dolphins," in J. R. Norman and F. C. Fraser, *Giant Fishes, Whales and Dolphins.* London: Putnam 1937. Pp. 201–361. (Still one of the best reviews of general information on dolphins. There have been a number of editions of this same work that are all good and some more recent than this date.)

Hershkovitz, Philip. *Catalog of Living Whales.* Washington, D.C.: United States National Museum Bulletin 246, 1966. 259 pp. (Not a narrative text, but useful especially in that it includes a large number of references to many kinds of dolphins.)

Kellogg, Remington. "Whales, Giants of the Sea," *The National Geographic Magazine* (1940), Vol. 77, No. 1, pp. 35–90. (Despite its age, still contains much useful information; the colored paintings by Else Bostelmann are especially useful even though some contain errors.)

Kellogg, Winthrop N. *Porpoises and Sonar.* Chicago: University of Chicago Press, 1961. 177 pp. (An interesting narrative text describing some of the early research on dolphin echolocation.)

Nishiwaki, Masaharu. *Whales and Pinnipeds.* Tokyo: University of Tokyo Press, 1965. 439 pp. (To most of our readers this will be of little use because the text is in Japanese. However, the illustrations are very useful in making identifications—scientific names are included that most of us can read—and an English translation is in preparation.)

Norris, Kenneth S. (ed.). *Whales, Dolphins, and Porpoises.* Berkeley: University of California Press, 1966. 789 pp. (Contains a number of technical papers, some quite readable, on a variety of subjects having to do with dolphin research.)

Norris, Kenneth S. "The evolution of acoustic mechanisms in odontocete cetaceans," in *Evolution and Environment,* Ellen T. Drake, ed., New Haven: Yale University Press, 1968. Pp. 297–324. (An especially good summary of current research on dolphin echolocation.)

Norris, Kenneth S. "The echolocation of marine mammals," in Andersen, *op. cit.*, pp. 391–423. (Another good summary of current research on dolphin echolocation.)

Norris, Kenneth S., and John H. Prescott. *Observations on Pacific Cetaceans in Californian and Mexican Waters.* Berkeley: University of California Press, University of California Publications in Zoology (1961), Vol. 63, No. 4, pp. 291–402 and pls. 27–41. (Contains many good observations on dolphins and some useful photographs.)

Palmer, Ralph S. *The Mammal Guide.* Garden City, New York: Doubleday and Co., 1954. 384 pp. (Contains one of the better guides, with good illustrations, to the identification of dolphins and other cetaceans in American waters.)

Pilleri, G. (ed.). *Investigations on Cetacea.* Bern, Switzerland: Institute of Brain Anatomy, University of Bern, Vol. 1 (1969), 219 pp.; Vol. 2 (1970), 296 pp. (First two volumes of a continuing series containing technical articles by many authors on many subjects dealing with Cetacea: articles include considerable information on dolphins, and much of it from observations made in the wild. Articles usually well illustrated.)

Poulter, Thomas C. "Marine mammals," in *Animal Communication; Techniques of Study and Results of Research,* Thomas A. Sebeok, ed. Bloomington: Indiana University Press, 1968. Pp. 405–465. (Of primary value for its bibliography, which is extensive on the subject of production of sound by dolphins and other marine mammals.)

Rice, Dale W. "Cetaceans," in *Recent Mammals of the World: A Synopsis of Families,* Sydney Anderson and J. Knox Jones, eds. New York: The Ronald Press, 1967, pp. 291–324. (An excellent summary of general information on dolphins and other cetaceans, briefly stated.)

Rice, Dale W., and Victor B. Scheffer. *A List of the Marine Mammals of the World.* Washington, D.C.: U.S. Fish and Wildlife Service, Special Scientific Report—Fisheries, No. 579 (1968), 16 pp. (A valuable list of marine mammals and their distribution; not a narrative text.)

Ridgway, Sam H. "The bottlenosed dolphin in biomedical research," in *Methods of Animal Experimentation,* William I. Gay, ed., New York: Academic Press, 1968. Vol. 3, pp. 387–446. (A valuable summary of information on the care and handling of dolphins.)

Ridgway, Sam H. *Mammals of the Sea: Biology, Medicine and Husbandry.*

Fort Lauderdale, Florida: Charles C Thomas, Publisher. (At this writing this book was scheduled for publication in 1971. The title is tentative, but indicates the scope of the book which will include invited chapters on many subjects related to dolphin biology by a number of authors who are specialists in their respective fields.)

Scammon, Charles M. *The Marine Mammals of the North-Western Coast of North America, Described and Illustrated: Together With An Account of the American Whale-Fishery.* San Francisco: John H. Carmany and Co., 1874, 319 pp. (A classic that contains much firsthand information on dolphins that is still valuable. Several reprint editions by different publishers have appeared in recent years.)

Slijper, E. J. *Whales.* London: Hutchinson and Co., 1962. 475 pp. (Originally published in Dutch; there is also an American edition. Contains general information on cetaceans, some of which is outdated.)

Tavolga, William N. (ed.). *Marine Bio-acoustics.* New York: Pergamon Press, Vol. 1 (1964), 413 pp.; Vol. 2 (1967), 353 pp. (Includes chapters on sound production by cetaceans.)

Tomilin, A. G. *Mammals of the U.S.S.R. and Adjacent Countries.* Jerusalem: Israel Program for Scientific Translations, 1967. Part 9 (Cetacea), 717 pp. (A compilation of worldwide data. Originally published in Russian.)

C. *From time to time we are asked for sources of recorded dolphin sounds. We can recommend the following which at this writing are still available:*

Schevill, William E., and William A. Watkins. *Whale and Porpoise Voices.* Woods Hole, Massachusetts: Woods Hole Oceanographic Institution, 1962. (Phonograph record of sounds, recorded almost entirely in the wild, from a variety of species including the bottlenosed dolphin. Package includes a useful 24-page illustrated booklet. By far the best general record available at this writing.)

A selection of sounds produced by captive bottlenosed dolphins, produced by the authors and narrated by Nicholas R. Hall, has been prepared. Available both in cassette and reel style from Biological Systems, Inc., P. O. Box 26, St. Augustine, Florida.

Index

Italic page numbers indicate illustrations.